Touching the Pulse: Worship and Our Diverse World

edited by Leslie Griffiths

To Ron and Gwen Ashman
who got me started

Also available in this series:

Worship and Where we Live edited Sandy Williams

Worship and Where we Work edited Bernard Braley

Stainer & Bell

First published in 1998 by Stainer & Bell Ltd
23 Gruneisen Road, London N3 1DZ

© 1998 Stainer & Bell Limited

British Library Cataloguing-in-Publication Data
A catalogue record for this book is available from the British Library

ISBN 0 85249 832 2

Cover photograph courtesy of Pictor International – London

Printed in Great Britain by Galliards, Great Yarmouth

Introduction

When I learned that my first appointment as a Methodist minister was to be in Haiti I was filled with keen anticipation. Denis Wheatley had given us a lurid picture of the cruel barbarities of Voodoo; I'd just read Graham Greene's classic *The Comedians*; everyone had heard of the poverty of the Western hemisphere's poorest nation; and I had been one of the millions who'd seen the amazing Whicker's World interview with Dr François (PapaDoc) Duvalier on BBC television. A job in Haiti was something I could really get my teeth into. I'd got a bundle of qualifications and considered myself God's gift to the world. Lucky old Haiti!

Well, of course, the truth turned out to be very different. Because of a crisis within the Church, I ended up with responsibility for dozens of scattered rural churches instead of the safe city appointment I'd been led to expect. I couldn't speak a sentence in the local Créole language and didn't have a clue about Haitian culture. I soon learned. With my mouth firmly closed and my ears wide open, I spent several months just learning about the wealth of indigenous liturgical material which uneducated Haitian people somehow managed to bring out of their collective experience. Their spirituality was profound, their language and earthy metaphors bristled with life, while their music and art were vivid and full of colour. This was the time when the Vatican Council was giving impetus to such notions as inculturation, the vernacularisation of the liturgy and the preferential option for the poor. All this led to an explosion of creativity. Calypso, drums and pipes, the Créole language – all these were brought into church for the first time.

Haiti taught me that the poor may be poor and the illiterate may well not be able to read or write but their capacity to worship is in no way diminished or restricted because of that. Since those faraway years in the Caribbean, I've had occasion to travel extensively in Africa and the Americas. I never visit a new land now without expecting to discover fresh and down-to-earth ways on the part of the local people of giving voice to the questions, the anxieties, the yearnings and the praise which are on their hearts and minds. The long struggle against apartheid in South Africa, the march towards nationhood in Eritrea, the never-ending civil war in Angola, the daily experience of dictatorship in Haiti, the discovery of the spirituality of people of other faiths, the ever deepening realisation of the horrors of the Holocaust – all these get turned into prayer and give shape to liturgical material in a way that is often deeply moving and almost always possessed of an immediacy which is arresting. The best of such devotion is never otherworldly or escapist; it avoids both Karl Marx's famous dictum about religion being an opium for the people and also Sigmund Freud's dismissal of religion as being an infantile delusion. It seems far too rugged and earthed to deserve either of these comments.

I've wanted to bring some of these riches together in this book. That's one of its objectives. But there are two others. Firstly, I've wanted to extend the range of places we might pray for. I can't think how often I've sat in church when intercessory prayers are offered and had to content myself with some generalised prayers about fairly predictable places. With this in mind, I've tried to write some meditations which get "unfashionable" places onto the agenda. I've tried to tease out some themes which, whilst originating in Bosnia or Bulgaria or wherever, can be of more general use too. I hope some of what follows will paint lots of pictures without becoming mere catalogues of information. And yet the information is important too. "Dear Lord, bless Bosnia," isn't quite enough.

The other thing I've wanted to do is to bring into the focus of prayer some everyday subjects from other parts of the world just for the joy of it. We're used to thinking of apples and pears, cabbages and turnips, in our Harvest Festival services. We don't often get to hear about mangos and pawpaw, cassava and sweet potato. And who has ever thought of charcoal?

I hope readers will use the material which follows in whatever way suits them. Perhaps bits and pieces will lend themselves to occasional use in public worship. Or house groups may be the most appropriate setting. Some items may feed someone's devotional life or lend themselves to meditation and prayer. I don't feel in the least bit possessive of any of the things I've written. Hack them about, take the bits you like, work them in to themes you're developing. Be my guest. I just hope this little book will extend people's repertoire, open their eyes to the big wide world we live in, and stimulate a response of prayer and worship which will in some way honour God and glorify his name.

A very long period of gestation has preceded the appearance of this little book. I feel I must offer profound apologies to my co-contributors, Sandy Williams and Bernard Braley, who had every right to expect the completion of a task we'd all expected long before now. The trouble was that I became President of the Methodist Conference and my life ceased to be mine for two or three years. I've been pretty close to giving up on this project more than once but Bernard Braley, champion of religious and liturgical publishing, has cajoled, coaxed, strong-armed me into continuing. I want to pay tribute to him here for a lifetime of commitment to excellence in the field of publishing and a wonderful example of just how the priesthood of all believers can best be expressed in a layman's working life. His own volume in this series is as good a monument to these sterling qualities as could be hoped for. My thanks are also due to those at Stainer & Bell who've done so much donkey work with persistence and good humour even when they knew they were dealing with a difficult author who didn't seem able to send them very much that was either tidy or organised.

Finally, let me say how much in debt I am to the congregations at Hinde Street, Golders Green and Wesley's Chapel. Wonderfully multi-ethnic and many-hued, these churches have given me the privilege of friendship and inspiration over many years. In fact, I don't have to travel the world to find vibrant and creative devotional material. Every Sunday for well over ten years, I seem to have stood in front of people who are a microcosm of the diverse world we live in. They have been my mentors in ways they probably couldn't guess at.

Leslie Griffiths
Wesley's Chapel, London
August 1998

Contents

THE ELEMENTS

One Creator
One Diverse Creation

1 Creation

In the beginning God made the world,
The overarching heavens and the teeming earth;
Made all that is
        out of an aching void;
Gave shape and form
        to a seething mass;
Shone light into the deepest darkness
        penetrating its thick obscurity;
And God took pleasure from all that had been made.

In the beginning God made the world,
Covered its surface with water;
Punctuated oceans with dry land;
Revealed the shape of continents,
        the mass of Asia
        the curves of Africa
        the length of the Americas
        the Antipodes
        and Europe
All were called into being by a God
Who took pleasure from all that had been made.

From the beginning God filled the earth
With everything that lives and breathes,
Everything that grows and sighs,
All that crawls, flies, swims or walks,
All that cries, laughs, sings, or speaks;
God made them all, mothered and fathered them,
Cherished them,
And took delight from all that had been made.

Let us lift up our hearts;
And give our thanks
For the splendour and the mystery of creation;
For the daily rising of the sun,
For the nightly rising of the moon,
For the life with which we share this planet.

Let us lift up our hearts;
And give thanks
For our history,
For the factors that have formed us,
For the men and women who have moulded us,
For the great and the mighty,
        the makers and the shakers,
        the wheelers and the dealers;
And also for the forgotten ones of history, the unrecorded ones,
For all those roses born to blush unseen and waste their fragrance
        on a desert air.

Let us lift up our hearts;
And give our thanks
For the sheer variety of human life,
The spectrum spread of our ethnic groupings,
        the sound and idiom of the languages we speak,
        the insights of human culture,
        the wealth of people's experience,
The infinite diversity of the rainbow people of God.

Let us lift up our hearts;
And give our thanks
For those who still inspire and stir up hope;
For prophets, martyrs and poets,
Preachers and philosophers,
Healers and peacemakers,
Rebels and reformers,
And everyone who goes on believing in good
Even when evil seems to flourish.

In the beginning, eternal God, you made the world
And all that is.
Today we acknowledge the miracle of creation
Not as an act trapped in the past,
Something accomplished with the fatal note of a historic finality,
But as a process that continues.
We rejoice that you still bring order out of chaos.
We pray that we may discern your creative presence
In our heaving, wonderful, suffering, glorious, tragic, many-splendoured,
pathetic world.
We pray that we may always remember
That our world is your world.
And as you have taken pleasure and delight in it
Since its very creation,
So too may we.

Leslie Griffiths

2 Creating Word

Creating Word,
bringing the world into being;
for the starred sky and the songbird that tell of your being,
for peoples diverse in colour and culture,
made in your image, speaking in many tongues, –
we praise you.

Help us to see you at work in the world:
May our lives tell the Good News.

Living word,
seen and heard in Jesus, teacher and storyteller,
speaking words of healing and forgiveness,
standing silent in the face of hatred and lies,
crying out on the cross –
we believe in you.

Help us to hear the cries of the world today:
May our lives tell the Good News.

Breath of the Spirit,
rushing wind and still small voice,
challenging, changing, making connections,
creating community, encouraging hope,
come among us, inspire us –
we need you.

Help us to communicate your love:
May our lives tell the Good News. Amen.

3 The Word in the World

May the words we speak
and all we think
be pleasing to you,
God our strength and our redeemer.

Creating Word, God from the beginning,
bringing into being all that lives and moves,
we pray for our busy world, a Babel
in need of your Word which brings order out of chaos;
we pray for nations at war,
communities divided by ideologies and insults,
by the graffiti-scrawled walls of cities
by the babble of the airwaves;
we pray for the pain of people who want to communicate
but can't understand each other.
We pray for a world waiting for the Word

May the words we speak
and all we think
be pleasing to you,
God our strength and our redeemer.

Living and loving Word, God with us,
we pray for those finding words to share their faith;
for all preachers – of long experience and those still learning;
for those who have inspired us,
and those who encourage others, and set standards,
for tutors, administrators, course writers;
for worship leaders and musicians;
for all who help worship to happen, week by week;
for the whole people of God, in our daily lives.
We pray for those who preach the Word.

May the words we speak
and all we think
be pleasing to you,
God our strength and our redeemer.

Still small voice, God who speaks in the silence,
as well as in the rushing mighty wind,
we pray for those who listen:
for the people in the pew and in the street,
and those who hesitate in the church doorway;
small children with words washing over their heads,
and the young full of catch-phrases and questions;
the housebound, ministered to by tapes,
and the lonely, listening to the radio;
the deaf, hearing with their eyes,
and those overwhelmed by words
but inspired by sign and symbol;
for people who work all week and need
nourishment and encouragement on Sunday:
we pray for those who listen.

May the words we speak
and all we think
be pleasing to you,
God our strength and our redeemer.

Word at work in the World, God who knows no frontiers,
we pray for those who share the Good News
in many different lands:
from high pulpits and under palm-leaf shelters,
in huge congregations, on street corners,
and where two or three are gathered together;
for those who use their mother tongue,
and those who struggle with words that don't come easily;
in situations where church-going is a sign of respectability,
and where the gospel is seen as subversive;
for those who, speaking out, risk their freedom and their lives.
We pray for preachers world-wide.

**May the words we speak
and all we think
be pleasing to you,
God our strength and our redeemer.**

Creative Word, living Word,
at work in the world, still small voice,
word of encouragement, rebuke,
challenge, hope,
we pray for those who have not yet heard,
and for all called to share the Good News.

**May the words we speak
and all we think
be pleasing to you,
God our strength and our redeemer.**

4   How can we praise you, living God

1 How can we praise you, living God,
   and celebrate this festival,
   when millions cry for daily bread
   whose hunger is perpetual?

2 Why do you let it happen, Lord?
   Are we mis-led, to think you good?
   Or are you helpless, after all,
   to feed them even if you would?

3 Or is it we, so self-absorbed,
   insensitive to poverty,
   who block love's course and leave your poor
   condemned to die in misery?

4 How can we praise you, living God?
   – Who doubt your power and righteousness;
   whose greed and paucity of love
   must make the earth a wilderness!

5 Great God, transform our politics;
   restrain our ruthless selfishness;
   by Christ's self-sacrifice in us
   display your love's effectiveness.

6 May we yet reap love's harvest, Lord,
   of justice and sufficiency,
   and all be fed and spirit-filled,
   with praise increasing endlessly.

Alan Gaunt
Tunes: HURSLEY, also known as GROSSER GOTT,
or STILLORGAN [L.M.]

5 Big Blue Planet

BIG BLUE PLANET

June Baker (1936–)

Big blue plan-et, swing-ing through the un-i-verse,

big blue plan-et; what can it be? what can it be? It's the plan-et

VERSE 4: REPEAT

V.5

earth, it's the plan-et earth, it's the plan-et earth, it's the plan-et earth.

Big blue plan-et, swing-ing through the un-i-verse, God loves the

plan-et: loves the land and loves the sea, loves the land and loves the sea.

Loves the peo-ple, that's you and me, loves the peo-ple, that's you and me. We'll love it

too, it's our plan-et EARTH, we'll love it too, it's our plan-et EARTH.____

1 Big blue planet, swinging through the universe,
   big blue planet; what can it be? what can it be?
   It's the planet earth, it's the planet earth,
   it's the planet earth, it's the planet earth.

2 Big blue planet, swinging through the universe,
   big blue planet; what can we see? what can we see?
   The great blue waters and the great green land,
   the great blue waters and the great green land.

3 God's blue planet, swinging through the universe,
   God's blue planet, what does God see? what does God see?
   All the people of the world, all the people of the world,
   all the people of the world, all the people of the world.

4 Poor blue planet, swinging through the universe,
   poor blue planet:
   water all soiled, land all spoiled.
   water all soiled, land all spoiled.
   And the people are sad, and the people are sad,
   and the people are sad, and the people are sad.

5 Big blue planet, swinging through the universe,
   God loves the planet:
   loves the land and loves the sea,
   loves the land and loves the sea.
   Loves the people, that's you and me,
   loves the people, that's you and me.
   We'll love it too, it's our planet EARTH,
   we'll love it too, it's our planet EARTH.

June Baker

6 Let us praise the Lord
(based on Psalm 136)

1st Voice: Let us with a gladsome mind
Praise the Lord who is so kind:

All: **God's own mercies aye endure,
Ever faithful, ever sure.**

1st Voice: Ours a world so richly blessed,
Flowers sprang up at God's behest:

2nd Voice: Hibiscus, bougainvillea, frangipani, oleander,
Poinsettia, ixora, jasmine, jacarinda,
in flames, wreaths, constellations of breathtaking colour;

All: **God's own mercies aye endure,
Ever faithful, ever sure.**

1st Voice: And trees grew in abundance too,

2nd Voice: Banyan, breadfruit, rubber and mahogany,
Bay rum, nutmeg, cinammon and cotton tree,
Calabash, flamboyant, buttercup and tulip too,
Arching, stretching, flaming to the skies.

All: **God's own mercies aye endure,
Ever faithful, ever sure.**

1st Voice: And so much more,

2nd Voice: Coffee, in groves hiding from the sun,
Tea, on plantations clothing entire hillsides,
Cocoa, in large red pods on old gnarled trees.

All: **God's own mercies aye endure,
Ever faithful, ever sure.**

1st Voice: And still the creation shows God's providence,

2nd Voice: Sugar cane and spice,
Sisal, indigo, cashew and groundnut,
Figs and dates and coconuts too.

All: **God's own mercies aye endure,
Ever faithful, ever sure.**

1st Voice: And so many luscious fruit and lusty vegetables,

2nd Voice: Bananas and mangos, kiwifruit and soursop,
guava, lychee, pawpaw and pineapple;
Plaintain and rice, millet and corn,
Sweet potatoes, carrots, cassava and beans.

1st Voice: All things living God doth feed,
With full hands supplied their need.

All: **God's own mercies aye endure,
Ever faithful, ever sure.**

Leslie Griffiths

Many Peoples

Many Cultures

Many Histories

7 China

Sleeping dragon, unknown force,
Enigma shrouded in mystery,
Lurking at the edge of our minds
though dominating the world we live in.

8,700 miles of coastline,
12,400 miles of land frontier,
A billion and a quarter inhabitants,
God's own children every one,
Worshipping and reverencing in their various ways;
Taoists,
Confucianists,
Buddhists,
As well as the followers of Christ and Mohamed.

China stretches away behind its bamboo curtain,
A land shaped by vast mountain ranges,
Himalayas, Kunhun Shan, Tian Shan,
and the sacred mount Tai Shan.
It's a world within a world
criss-crossed by the snaking meanderings
of the Yangtze, Mekun, and Yellow rivers,
its landscape marked by deserts and rice paddies,
studded with sprawling hyperactive cities
Shanghai, Beijing, Shenyang.
This is a land ruled by old men who still dream dreams
of the day when Formosa/Taiwan
will be gathered again
along with Tibet and Hong Kong
under the wing of the mother land
in their people's republic
sleeping dragon, unknown force,
enigma shrouded in mystery.

China is wellspring of culture and civilisation,
writing, art, philosophy and ceramics.
But also the brutality of its red guards,
and the still reverberating, chilling
events of Tianaman Square.

How do we pray for a land so huge and impenetrable?
How focus on its people's hopes and fears,
or the ways it might enrich us all,
when we feel so distant, overwhelmed
by its inscrutability and strange otherness?

Perhaps prayer would flow most freely from the vasty deeps
of themes thrown up in China;
our thoughts might most creatively
gather round metaphors given birth
by the events of her recent history.

China gave us the idea of the **long march**,
that trek in the early thirties in search of a new beginning,
a pilgrimage of hope begun by 100,000,
accomplished by a mere surviving 8,000.
We pray for all the Chinese people on their present-day long march into the modern age, in search of
economic reforms and a shaping role in the international community, that this may be accomplished by all
its people and reach the goal of freedom, justice, and peace.

From China came the idea of the **great leap forward**,
the possibility of emerging from a shrouded past
into a bright new day with energy and a zest for living.
We pray for China in these times of great transition, that her people may indeed leap forward, hope in their
hearts, into a future they all want to embrace.

China replaced ancient and corrupt dynastic rule with a **people's republic**.
Mao Zedung's words, uttered on October 1st 1949 at the birth of
this brave new world, should still ring in the ears of all people:
"Today," he said, "China enters into the family of nations who love peace and freedom."
We pray that this may indeed be the case for the sake of all the people who form the republic and, indeed,
for the sake of the whole human family.

China gave us the idea of a **cultural revolution**,
where renewal and revival
never settle or grow stale;
where there is an ongoing effervescence
harnessing people's energy
stimulating new achievements,
redefining the horizons of hope.
We pray that we may make this metaphor our own,
we who hang on to the known and fear the future,
we who refuse to take risks,
and draw on the capital of our parents' yesterday
without investing too much in our children's tomorrow.

Sleeping dragon, unknown, mysterious, enigmatic,
China can teach us all so much.

God bless China,
Her leaders and her people.
May she be a blessing to us all
And pleasing in your sight.

O Lord, our rock and our redeemer. **Amen.**

Leslie Griffiths

The eyes of the merciful Lord are upon me,
For my mind's eyes can see so clearly.
No dark clouds separate us.

Let enemies come and blindfold me,
Or burn my sight with painful torches.
The all-seeing Lord will protect me,
Lending me his unfailing sight.

Slumber not, my caring Lord,
Sleep not, my merciful God.
Do not turn your face away,
Though my look be so ungainly
And my body frail.

Rejoice, for the Lord sees me,
His sight kindly restores me,
Now and on Resurrection Day.

A "psalm" written for worship by Chinese Christians
in difficult times.

Angels on high, strengthen me,
Walk us through this Dragon Hill.
This land toss and turn and roar;
Calm its brave heart, still our fear.

Part of a hymn written during a time when Chinese
Christians were being persecuted.

May God raise up more workers after his own
heart and revive the church throughout China.
May he awaken our sleepy souls. We sometimes
pray with tears.

From a member of a small church in Hebei.

8 Marsh Arabs

Mesopotamia, fertile land between the Tigris and Euphrates,
Paradise, garden of Eden,
The beginnings of time and the place of innocence.
Bliss was it at the dawn of human history when to be alive was very heaven.

Mesopotamian marshlands, all these centuries later,
drained and changed beyond all recognition;
a people's culture wantonly destroyed,
whole populations terrorised and put to flight.
Fearful is it now to be there and for most their life is veritable hell.

Marshland arabs have suffered unimaginably.
Saddam Hussein's victims are victims still.
Half a million have fled across the Iranian border,
Unknown numbers have been tortured, chased, beaten, killed.
Dairy products and fish harvests are no more.
The help and interest of the big wide world are hard to maintain.
Another needy people to forget about.

But oblivion mustn't swallow up these people, making them another sacrifice to Moloch.
Our prayers and practical help must continue till the last syllable of available time.
Western businesses are jostling for pole position for the expected resumption of
commercial activity with Saddam Hussein's Iraq.
We dare not allow the question, "Who cares about his victims?" ever once to be formulated.

God cares.
God's children care.
AMAR* cares.
Care carried on the wings of prayer
To our brothers and sisters in the garden of Eden
Can wrap them in the arms of our love.
As an Arab proverb puts it so well:
"What comes from the lips reaches the ears;
What comes from the heart reaches the heart."
So be it.

*AMAR is a refugee charity named after an Iraqi orphanage. It has worked tirelessly
and fearlessly alongside the marshland Arabs in their toughest times.*

Leslie Griffiths

9 The Karen Hill People

Out of the one country called Burma so many peoples, spread in a spectrum of ethnic and tribal groups across the Chin, Kachin, Kayah, Mon, Rakhine, Shan and Karen peoples. The Karen people predominate in the long and narrow strip of land that snakes off towards the deep south along a border shared with Thailand. One in five of them are Christians, a level not reached in any of Burma's other tribes. They are also among the most persecuted. We lift them up in our prayers.

Lord hear us.
Lord graciously hear us.

The Yadana gas pipeline, constructed in defiance of world opinion and international protest, is being built by the French Total company and financed by the American Unocal company. Another line from Yetagun to the Andaman Sea is being built by Texaco. This is greatly resented by the Karen people whose land is being roughshod over for the profit of these multinational operations. We hold up the Karen hill people in our prayers.

Lord hear us.
Lord graciously hear us.

The Karen people have dared to show resistance to the SLORC* military government which has ruled Burma since it took power in 1990 after free and fair elections. The legitimately elected head of state, Nobel Peace Prize Winner Aung San Suu Kyi, has gone on living in Burma since the poll, most of the time under house arrest. Her example shines like a beacon in the darkness that surrounds her. The Karen people meanwhile have paid dearly for their temerity. We hold them up in our prayers.

Lord hear us.
Lord graciously hear us.

The Karen people are used as forced labour or as porters; they are virtual slaves, unpaid, oppressed, denied their basic human rights. Village girls are raped by SLORC agents, Karen houses are under threat of confiscation, schools are not allowed to use the ethnic language of everyday life. 18,000 Karen people have been driven over the Thai border into a miserable exile. We hold them up in our prayers.

Lord hear us.
Lord graciously hear us.

Eternal God, wonderful in counsel, excellent in wisdom, we pray for the representatives of the nations who have been called to the task of laying firm foundations for the peace of the world. Inspire their minds, enlarge their vision, direct their councils, that humble and wise, fearless and unfaltering, they may stand and work for righteousness and truth.

We pray also for the peoples in whose names they speak and also those who have no opportunity to speak, people like those of the Karen hill country; raise the minds of men and women everywhere above the mists of suspicion and hatred into the light of trust and goodwill, that justice and mercy may be established among all nations.

Through Jesus Christ our Lord.

Amen.

* SLORC = State Law and Order Restoration Council.

Leslie Griffiths

10 A Psalm for South Africa

This was written for the 25th Anniversary of the South African Council of Churches. Before using it, take time to familiarise yourself with the explanatory notes printed at the end.

Praise the name of the Lord
Praise God who has given us hope!
Praise God, you people living in the land of Africa,
in the streets and farms of our God.

From high blue skies to hot deep mines,
from dusty deserts to towering peaks,
from grey littered streets to green fields and forests,
from oceans edged with warm white beaches,
to concrete cities and long black highways:
the Lord's will is sovereign.

Sing glory to the name of God who inspires hope
Because God has called South Africa to be saved.
We have learned for ourselves that God is great,
that our Lord surpasses all other gods.

The Lord struck down the idols of apartheid,
and denounced pride and racism.
The Lord sent signs and wonders against the false gospel,
and forced change upon its officials.

Where is the Special Branch? Where are their "panel beaters?"
Where are the pagan idols, the pass books and the casspirs?
What befell the handcuffs and the sjamboks?
Where are the bombs that wiped out the buildings,
that took our eyes, our limbs, our lives?
Where is the Group Areas Act: what happened to Influx Control?
These were the violent signs of powerlessness,
of a god of make believe, a power which could not endure.

O Lord, your name endures for ever!
Lord, your memory is ever fresh.
For you have vindicated your children
And honoured those who served God's people.

Woza Albert! Viva Sobukwe! Long live Steve Biko!
Hail Helen Joseph and Lilian Ngoyi! Amandla Chris Hani!
Remember "The Message" and the "Kairos Document"!
Praise God for those who gave us hope when all seemed hopeless!
This is the legacy put into the hands of our people,
This is the legacy given us by the Lord.

For we were a shattered, scattered people,
On the pavements of New York and Amsterdam,
By the waters of London and Geneva,
We sought to sing our songs, but wept.
They welcomed us under the starry skies of Somafco and Dakawa,
On the streets of Lusaka and Harare,
But how could we sing the Lord's song in a strange land?

Then we heard the promise of the Lord:
"I will bring your offspring from the east,
and gather you from the west."
To the north I will say, "Give them up"
and to the south: "Do not hold them."
Bring back my children from far away.

This is the Lord's doing and it is wonderful to behold!
Glory be to the Father, and to the Son, and to the Holy Spirit;
As it was in the beginning, is now, and shall be for ever. Amen.

Explanatory notes

1 Special branch: the feared security police.
2 "Panel Beating" was the nickname given to the torture of those in detention.
3 "Casspirs" are armoured cars used by the police and the army.
4 "Sjamboks" are hide whips.
5 Chief Albert Luthuli, a Congregationalist, was President of the ANC, and a Nobel Prize winner.
6 Robert Sobukwe (like Mandela, a Methodist) was the leader of the Pan Africanist Congress.
7 Steve Biko was the young visionary leader of the Black Consciousness Movement, killed in detention.
8 Helen Joseph and Lilian Ngoyi were friends in the struggle. Helen was banned for decades.
9 Chris Hani, a leader of the South African Communist Party was assassinated in 1993.
10 "The Message" and the "Kairos Document" were prophetic church pronouncements repudiating apartheid.
11 Somafco and Dakawa, camps for refugees in Tanzania.

11 Active Love

Written in thanksgiving for the lives and work of President Nelson Mandela and Archbishop Desmond Tutu.

1 Active love, not fearful frenzy,
   is the path that we pursue,
   counterblast to alienation,
   struggle making all things new.
   Facing up to common conflict,
   meeting arrogance with prayer,
   seeking to be one with Jesus,
   dignified amid despair.

2 Torture, fear and desecration
   paint the canvas of our lives;
   but the picture, deeply woven,
   demonstrates that love survives.
   Systems that would seek to scar us,
   mould us blindly to their trends,
   we will overthrow with kindness,
   not be subject to their ends.

3 We will take the cross of Jesus
   into every sphere of life,
   we will stand for peace and justice,
   we will not succumb to strife.
   We must meet this tribulation,
   live our lives, if need be, die;
   take no refuge in abstraction,
   take the cross and lift it high!

Andrew Pratt
Tune: BETHANY (Smart) [8.7.8.7.D. Trochaic]

12 Spirit of Peace

Happy and blest are the peace-makers,
living in the spirit, children of the light;
theirs is the harvest of true justice,
working in the spirit through the darkest night.

1 The spirit of peace is the spirit of danger,
   it gives of itself not to sacrifice others;
   it finds that of God in the foe and the stranger,
   and risks that our enemies can be our brothers,
       brothers, brothers.

   Chorus

2 The spirit of peace is the spirit of healing,
   it springs from the depths of our innermost centre;
   it opens our eyes to oppression's concealing
   and struggles that love into action may enter,
       enter, enter.

   Chorus

3 The spirit of peace is the spirit that's tender,
   it withers when violence clamours in shrillness;
   it blossoms when power begins to surrender,
   and rich are its fruits when there's freedom and stillness,
       stillness, stillness... stillness.

   Chorus

Alec Davison

17

13 Descendants of Abraham

This is a prayer from Hans Küng's *Judaism*. This book is one of a series devoted to a process deemed by Küng to be essential for the future well-being of the world, a process summed up thus:

- There can be no ongoing human society without a world ethic for the nations.
- There can be no peace among the nations without peace among the religions.
- There can be no peace among the religions without dialogue between the religions.

Hidden, eternal, unfathomable, all-merciful God,
beside you there is no other God.
You are great and worthy of all praise;
your power and grace sustain the universe.

God of all faithfulness without falsity, just and truthful,
You chose Abraham, your devout servant,
to be the father of many nations,
and you have spoken through the prophets.
Hallowed and praised be your name throughout the world.
May your will be done wherever people live.

Living and gracious God, hear our prayer;
our guilt has become great.
Forgive us children of Abraham our wars,
our enmities, our misdeeds towards one another.
Rescue us from all distress and give us peace.

Guardian of our destiny,
bless the leaders and rulers of the nations,
that they may not covet power and glory,
but act responsibly
for the welfare and peace of humankind.
Guide our religious communities and those set over them,
that they may not only proclaim the message of peace
but also show it in their lives.
And to all of us, and those who do not belong among us,
give your grace, mercy and all good things,
and lead us, God of the living,
on the right way to your eternal glory.

14 Sudan

The long civil war in Sudan has meant ordinary people living in constant fear and uncertainty. They desperately want peace and have asked Christians in Britain to pray for, and to call for, peace in Sudan.

Our Father,
   it is your
   universe,
   it is your will,
let us be at peace;
let the souls of your
   people be cool;
   you are our Father,
remove all evil
from our path.

16 We are One in Prayer

A Prayer from Ghana

O Lord, our heavenly Father,
You hear us praying here in Takoradi.
You hear our brothers [and sisters]
praying in Africa,
in Asia, in Australia,
in America and in Europe.
We are all one in prayer.
We praise and honour you,
and we beg you
that we may rightly carry out your commission;
to witness and to love,
in our church and throughout the whole world.
Accept our prayers graciously,
even when they are somewhat strange.
We praise you and pray to you
through Jesus Christ our Lord.
Amen.

15 Yoruba Poem

Enjoy the earth gently
Enjoy the earth gently
For if the earth is spoiled
It cannot be repaired
Enjoy the earth gently.

17 From Kenya

From the cowardice that dare not face new truth,
From the laziness that is contented with half truth,
From the arrogance that thinks it knows all truth,
Good Lord, deliver us.

18 From the Shipibo Indians in Peru

Our ancestors taught us to share what we gather in a day.
We must keep the forest as the home of animals but also for pure water and air.
The only reason it still exists is that we have taken care that it's not destroyed.
We need the trees for thatch, for medicines, and because they provide fruit.
The forest is our home.

19 From Guatemala

We love our land very much. Since these people tried to take
our land away we have grieved very much.
My grandfather used to cry bitterly and say: "In the past, no one person owned the land.
The land belonged to everyone."

Rigoberta Menchu

20 Thanksgiving

A Prayer from West Africa

Lord of lords,
Creator of all things,
God of all things,
God over all gods,
God of sun and rain,
You created the earth with a thought
and us
with Your breath.

Lord,
we brought in the harvest.
The rain watered the earth,
the sun drew cassava and corn
out of the clay.
Your mercy showered blessing after blessing
 over our country.
Creeks grew into rivers;
swamps became lakes.
Healthy fat cows graze on the green sea
of the savanna.
The rain smoothed out the clay walls,
the mosquitoes drowned in the high waters.

Lord,
the yam is fat like meat,
the cassava melts on the tongue,
oranges burst in their peels,
dazzling and bright.

Lord,
nature gives thanks;
Your creatures give thanks.
Your praise rises in us like the Volta.

Lord of lords,
Creator,
Provider,
we thank you in the name of Jesus Christ.
Amen.

21 Prayer of a Thai woman

Lord God most high, may we offer thee praise and thankfulness for thy loving kindness in letting us hear about thy precious Gospel. We are happy to be called Christians, and so make us all real ones. Grant us the power to feel thy presence among us. Cleanse our hearts and make them clear like crystals in order that we may see thee and that the Holy Spirit may dwell in us. Dear Lord... there are many friends of ours who have not heard about thy precious name nor have they seen thy light. Help us all to dedicate ourselves more in thy service and to shine for thee. Forgive us for being selfish and letting thy light grow dim. We ask these things in the name of the Great Lord Jesus Christ whose merits lift us from sin.

22 From Nigeria

O God of Abraham, God of Isaac and God of Jacob, the beginning and the end: without you we can do nothing. The great river is not big enough for you to wash your hands in. You have the yam and you have the knife; we cannot eat unless you cut us a piece. We are like little children who only wash their stomach when they bathe, leaving their back dry.

Chinua Achebe

23 Africa

God bless Africa!
        Guide her leaders, guard her children
        and give her peace.

Trevor Huddleston

24 South Africa

O God, the Father of all men and women,
we beseech thee so to inspire the people of this land
with the spirit of justice, truth, and love,
that in all our dealings one with another
we may show forth the deep bonds that hold us together in thee,
for the sake of Jesus Christ our Lord.

A Book of Common Prayer (South Africa)

25 Northern Ireland

I am perplexed, angry, hopeless, sick.
I want to turn my back, wash my hands, save myself, my family, get out.
But every time I turn to go,
there stands in my way a cross....
Lord, make me a child of hope, reborn from apathy, cynicism and despair,
ready to work for that new person
you have made possible by walking the way of the cross yourself.
I *do* have hope grounded on our victory over powers of evil, death itself.
That hope is focused on your kingdom,
breaking in on us now as light out of deep darkness.
And I do see signs of hope immediately around me.
I see a sign – flowers growing on a bombed-out site.
The sign – an empty cross. The burden, Lord, is yours.
Lord, I am a prisoner of hope! There *is* a life before death.

26 Prayer for the Rich

Lord, the world needs
this marvellous wealth which is youth.
Help young people.
They possess the inexhaustible wealth of the future...
Do not allow an easy life to corrupt them
Nor difficulties to quench their spirit.
Free them from the worst danger of all –
That of getting used to being
Old within themselves
And only young on the outside.

Dom Hélder Cámara

27 From Nicaragua

Free us, Lord,
because their parties did not free us.
They fool each other,
They exploit each other,
Their lies are repeated by thousands of radios,
Their slanders by every newspaper,
They have special workshops for making up those lies.
Those who say
"We shall dominate by means of propaganda,
Propaganda is with us."

"Because of the oppression of the poor
Because of the groans of the exploited
I will arise now"
Says the Lord,
"I will give them freedom because they sigh."
But the words of the Lord are clean words
They are not propaganda.

Ernesto Cardenal

28 Prayer of a Filipino

Lord, make us realize that our Christianity is like a rice field, that when it is newly planted, the paddies are prominent; but as the plants take root and grow taller, these dividing paddies gradually vanish, and soon there appears only one vast continuous field. So give us roots of love and make us grow in Christian fellowship and service, that thy will be done in our lives, through our Saviour, thy Son, Jesus Christ.

29 Philippines

Lord, in these times when we are about to lose hope and our efforts seem futile, grant that we may perceive in our hearts and minds the image of your resurrection which remains our only source of courage and strength, so that we may continue to face the challenges, and struggle against hardship and oppression born of injustice.

From a liturgy created for use by the people of one of the poorest slum areas in Manila.

30 From Uruguay

O God, may your Church discover, then identify, its life with groups of people who suffer injustice and remain unheard. May your Church be the voice of the voiceless. Let your Church find them, and struggle with them, and so find the way of your cross, and the way to true responsibility.

Emilio Castro (slightly amended)

31 United States of America

O God, who has bound us together in this bundle of life, give us grace to understand how our lives depend upon the courage, the industry, the honesty and the integrity of our fellow human beings, that we may be mindful of their needs, grateful for their faithfulness, and faithful in our responsibilities to them; through Jesus Christ our Lord.

Reinhold Niebuhr

32 God's Great Expectations

We have become complacent
in our structures and institutions.
We have been subtly diverted
from his will and purpose in our world.
We have selfishly interpreted his word
to fit our schemes and to carry out our own intents.
We have clutched at God to pacify and sustain us
even while we remain insensitive
to the suffering world about us.

"How long will you ignore
My oppressed and dispossessed children,
their cries for liberty and justice?"
our God is saying to us.

"Why are there people going hungry around you
while you abound in gifts from my hand?"
he asks insistently.

"You are my servants,
my representatives in a fractured world.
I can reach those sick, needy, loveless and
lonely creatures only through you.
This is the reason I have given you so much.
That you may share it with them."
Thus speaks the Lord.

Leslie Brandt

33 The Caribbean

The right hand of God is striking in our land
Striking out at envy, hate and greed.
Our selfishness and lust, our pride and deeds unjust
Are destroyed by the right hand of God.
The right hand of God is healing in our land,
Healing broken bodies, minds and souls.
So wondrous is its touch,
With love that means so much,
When we're healed by the right hand of God.
The right hand of God is planting in our land,
Planting seeds of freedom, hope and love,
In these Caribbean lands
Let his people all join hands
And be one with the right hand of God.

Patrick Prescod

34 Prayer for Peace

O bless this people, Lord, who seek their own face
under the mask and can hardly recognize it....
O bless this people that breaks its bond....
And with them, all the peoples of the North and South,
of East and West,
who sweat blood and sufferings,
and see, in the midst of these millions of waves
the sea swell of the heads of my people
and grant to them warm hands that they may clasp
the earth in a girdle of brotherly hands,
beneath the rainbow of thy peace.

Léopold Sédar Senghor (abridged)

35 Prayer for Peace

Let all dwellers on earth recognize
and know this basic truth:
we have not come into this world
for the sake of strife and division
(God forbid),
nor for the sake of hatred and envy,
provocation, and the shedding of blood
(God forbid);
rather, we have come into the world
in order to recognize and know thee.
Be thou blessed for ever.

Rabbi Nachman of Bratzlav

36 Carnival colours, sounds of all nations

CARNIVAL COLOURS (10.10.10.10.)

Hannah Daniels (1972–)

1 Carnival colours, sounds of all nations,
   brighten the drabness and ring in the air,
   fullness of fun and joy in creation
   offered to God in our thanks for his care.

2 Steel bands and dancers, loud reggae music,
   streamers and rainbows of love and delight,
   laughing together, smiles on our faces,
   God at the centre, rejoice in his sight!

3 Festival faces, joy of the children,
   adult divisions are swept clean away
   simply by love, uniting all races,
   heralding clearly the dawn of God's day.

Andrew Pratt

37 The Stranger

Reader 1:   There was more, far more than I knew to my sky.
The sky I knew
lay out above my roof-tops
and I thought I knew
every star in my sky.
But you came, stranger,
and told me of other roof-tops, other skies.
You showed me other stars
and a country without frontiers
of which I knew nothing.

Reader 2:   There was more, far more than I knew to my earth.
The gardens I knew
were full of apple-trees and cherries.
But you came, stranger,
and planted my garden
with palms and olive plants,
and showed me a force in the earth
of which I knew nothing.

Reader 3:   There was more, far more than I knew to my tongue.
My tongue used to sing
in its own special accent and dialect.
But you came, stranger,
with other sounds
and new words,
and taught me new songs
of which I knew nothing.

Reader 4:   There was more, far more than I knew to my skin.
Down my street have come people
of every hue
from ebony black to golden brown.
And you came, stranger,
opening up limitless horizons
and astonishing countries
of which I knew nothing.

All: There was a whole world on my doorstep.
You
and others
and God.
A whole world of which I knew nothing.

John Pritchard freely adapted from an anonymous French poem

38 A Czech Litany

When we're down and helpless
When lies are reigning
When fears and indifference are growing
     – May your kingdom come.

     When joy is missing
     When love is missing
     When unbelief is growing
       – May your kingdom come.

          To the sick and lonely
          To the imprisoned and tortured
            – May your kingdom come.

               Into the churches,
               Into our praying,
               Into our singing,
                  – May your kingdom come.

                    Into our hearts,
                    Into our minds,
                    Into our eyes,
                      – May your kingdom come.

                    Soon!

39 A Penitential Prayer from South Africa

You asked for our hands
    that we might use them for your purpose.
We gave them for a moment then withdrew them for the work was hard.

You asked for our mouths
    to speak out against injustice.
We gave you a whisper that we might not be accused.

You asked for our eyes
    to see the pain of poverty.
We closed them for we did not want to see.

You asked for our lives
    that you might work through us.
We gave a small part that we might not get too involved.

Lord, forgive us for our calculated efforts to serve you
    only when it's convenient for us to do so,
    only in those places where it's safe to do so, and
    only with those who make it easy to do so.

Father, forgive us
    renew us
    send us out
    as usable instruments
    that we might take seriously
    the meaning of your cross.

Through Jesus Christ our Lord. **Amen.**

40 Angola

Angola was born beautiful.
Its mighty rivers,
Grand panoramas,
Spectacular scenery
Conspire to offer habitat
To animals and birds of a bewildering variety.
Truly the Lord is in this swathe of Africa.

Angola has torn itself to shreds.
Destruction and decay,
Broken bridges,
Landmined roads,
Fallen trees
Combine to perpetuate the memory
Of internecine strife and fratricidal war.
Truly the Lord has been abandoned
In this lovely part of Africa.

Only bicycles can pass along the road
Between Cazombo and Luwawo.
Swampy paths
And daunting hills
Make even that so difficult.
Mazoze lies along the road,
Guerilla base for many years.
The fighters still are there
Retired now,
Living with their families,
In post-war anonymity.

A priest arrived one day,
The first for over thirty years.
The people of Mazoze had not received communion
Since before the Second Council.
Hoc est corpus meum was all the old remembered;
The language of an era dead and buried.
The mass is now re-done in Portuguese and tribal tongues,
But though the words are comprehensible
The act itself is strange.

When symbols lose their meaning,
And bread and wine their sense,
What can ravaged communities do to lift up their hearts,
To lift them to the Lord?
With what remembered wisdom do they give thanks and praise
To the Lord their God?
Or bless the one who comes in the name of the Lord,
The Lamb of God
Who takes away the sin of the world
And grants it peace?

It was God who brought the beauty of Angola into being
And loves it still.
Pray that the Angolan people may rediscover
Sacramental hope in the symbolism of sacrifice
And pure, unadulterated love.

Leslie Griffiths

41 East Timor

For a people and its bishop,
For Christians under fire
    through long years of persecution
    and almost unimaginable suffering.

Lord in your mercy
Hear our prayer.

For Bishop Carlos Belo,
    a shy, retiring, bookish man
    who stands up to dictators
    and carries the suffering of his people
    who preaches reconciliation and
        non-violence
    and wins the Nobel Prize for peace
    who shows Christ to the world

Lord in your mercy
Hear our prayer.

Bishop Carlos Belo of Dili remains largely
    unknown,
his people's suffering causes few ripples of
    interest or concern,
their enemies' military force continues to be
    buttressed by arms we send them,
200,000 lives have been snuffed out, a third of
    the entire population of East Timor.

Lord have mercy
Lord have mercy.

The Indonesian government is determined to
    keep East Timor;
    they invaded it when the Portuguese left,
    they annexed it,
    they've ignored repeated Security Council
        resolutions ordering them to withdraw,
    they've got away with their illegal rule for
        over 20 years.

Christ have mercy
Christ have mercy.

The best of East Timor's land has been
    expropriated for Indonesian settlers,
Jobs and careers have been kept for
    Indonesian immigrants,
Local people have been killed,
Their property and possessions are regularly
    ransacked,
Terror reigns and British guns ensure that this
    continues,
There have been repeated assassination
    attempts on Bishop Carlos Belo.

Lord have mercy
Lord have mercy.

Suffering, so much suffering,
For years, so many years,
With the world looking on,
    looking the other way,
    looking surprised.
The Church has spoken with muted voice,
The United Nations Organisation has watched
    its fine words spurned,
The West has its hands sullied and bloodied.

Lord, hasten the day when your will may be done
On earth as it is in heaven.

For the people of East Timor,
For Bishop Carlos Belo of Dili,
May there be hope and justice,
    reconciliation and justice,
    peace with justice,
May the people taste justice and savour it,
May those in power hunger and thirst after
    justice,
May justice grow in the land
Till it flows like a river to the sea.

May your will be done and that right soon
On earth as it is in heaven.

Leslie Griffiths

42　A Prayer for Justice in Trade

Buyers and sellers,
God, you know, in our country
these people are quite special,

but nobody can fool you,
neither the buyer nor those who sell.

It is not just a trifle over which
we can make merry.

There can be fraud whilst people are hungry.
Others pile up their riches.
God, whether we buy or sell,
let us stick to one thing.

We are quite willing to pay the
value of the goods,
but others should not overcharge.
We often pray for peace.
God, make peace here as well.

43　A Prayer from Uruguay

Lord, you placed me in the world to be its salt.
I was afraid of committing myself,
Afraid of being stained by the world.
I did not want to hear what "they" might say.
And my salt dissolved as if in water.
Forgive me Jesus.

Lord, you placed me in the world to be its light.
I was afraid of the shadows,
Afraid of the poverty.
I did not want to know other people.
And my light slowly faded away.
Forgive me Jesus.

Lord, you placed me in the world to live in the community.
Thus you taught me to love,
To share in life,
To struggle for bread and for justice,
Your truth incarnate in my life.
So be it, Jesus.

Peggy M. de Cuehlo

44 El Salvador

Even in peace time
The most violent country on earth.
Memories bulging,
Hatred and fear welling within,
Hope tentative, fragile, scarred.

Whole communities were crushed by government troops
In the thirteen bloody years of war.
Bombs dropped on unsuspecting villages,
Soldiers rushed in firing indiscriminately.
They poisoned the water;
Slaughtered the animals;
Raped the girls;
Tied wood to women, doused them with petrol,
And turned them into human torches;
They cut open the bellies of pregnant women;
Sliced children in two;
Or tossed them and caught them on the points of their bayonets
Like a cheap fairground trick.

Seventy thousand died;
A million and a half peasants were displaced;
All this in a population of five million people.
Grim, ghastly, dirty stuff.

Now the survivors have a voice in parliament;
And they may even make a majority next time round.
But when will their wounds,
Mental and spiritual,
Be healed?
And how do those who inflicted these horrors
Live with their consciences?
Is a future possible
After such trauma?

The voice and life of Oscar Romero still strike home.
His words were clear enough.
To soldiers on the rampage he urged:
"When you hear the voice of a man commanding you to kill,
Remember instead the voice of God:
'Thou shalt not kill.'
I beseech you,
I beg,
I command you,
Stop this repression."

Within days he too was dead,
Another victim.
Another martyr.
A symbol of hope.
May he rest eternally.

And may his words echo from the silence of his grave.
May his people discover peace,
Discover it and cherish it,
And blossom in abundant living
Under the protection of its giver,
The God of a peace
That passes our imaginings,
That answers our deepest yearnings
And brings us home at the last
With great rejoicing.

Leslie Griffiths

45 Peace in Croatia

The day we heard that tanks
were on their way to Zagreb
we gathered, like every Thursday, for prayer.
Only this time there was no chit-chat,
no exchange of news,
no laughter among old friends.
We waited for prayers to start in silence.

We started by reading some psalms,
and suddenly the word PEACE
fell on our ears
weighty, thick and sweet,
like honey dripping from a spoon.

How often and how glibly had we uttered it:
I leave you peace, my peace I give you,
the peace of the Lord be with you always,
grant us peace.

But now we know:
peace is a word you can eat
like bread and butter.
It's a word you can hold in your lap
like a purring cat.
It's a word you can bask in
like spring sunshine.

And when we parted
we were pregnant with peace.

Sanja Matešic

As a child Sanja Matešic lived in London and New
York. She now lectures in the University of Zagreb.

46 War Shoes

When you put on heavy shoes
Brave clogs
Man's boots, war shoes
Unthinkingly you simply
Grab a rifle
And you set off
Down the muddy road.
When time comes for the gun-barrels to speak
Days of heroism, nights of chivalry,
When the foreign army floods the country
Causing destruction and misdeeds
The situation has to be dealt with
Then you cruise your homeland by foot
So your shoes are fighting alongside you
In war, they are worth much to you
For you to play a shining role.

Radovan Karadzic

47 God of the world's great cities

STALHAM (7.6.7.6.8 8.)

Mervyn Horder (1910–1997)

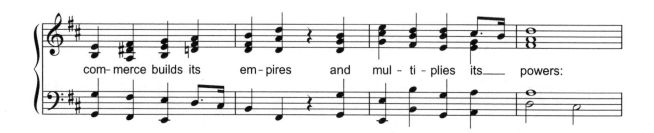

1 God of the world's great cities
with all their soaring towers,
as commerce builds its empires
and multiplies its powers:
this is the earth that Jesus trod;
do not abandon us, O God!

2 God of the crushed and broken
whose burdens Jesus bore,
in park and street and subway
you seek the hopeless poor:
still come to find them and to save
whose city is their lifelong grave.

3 God of the friends and neighbours
whose pleasures Jesus knew,
whose births and deaths and weddings
bring tangled thoughts of you:
in you they live and grow and move;
O let them taste your total love!

4 God of the proud and mighty
when crime or folly rules
remove earth's vicious tyrants,
restrain its godless fools:
grant those you keep in their high place
to love your truth, and know your grace.

5 God of the struggling remnant
baptized to bear that name
which at the end of all things
shall stand alone, supreme:
O help your church, by your strong hand,
confessing Christ, in Christ to stand.

6 God of the dawning kingdom,
while human wealth decays
you build a different city
of pure and lasting praise:
here let your people live, O Lord,
in Christ refashioned and restored.

Christopher Idle

48   Hebron

Dear Lord and Father of us all,

We pray for Hebron and for all who live there:

tens of thousands of Palestinians,
a few hundred Jews.

We remember the suffering of countless families, Arabs and Jews, in a city that's been such a flashpoint for sectarian violence over so many generations.

We give thanks for Abraham, – father-figure for Jews, Moslems and Christians alike, who lies buried within the ancient walls of Hebron. Remind us of:

> – his faith,
> – his readiness to do your will,
> – his ability to put his own plans on one side and
> – to follow in your way wherever it might lead.

Give us courage to be insipired by the example of Abraham; may his voice speak across the centuries; and may peace flourish in Hebron, the Holy Land, in our hearts and throughout the whole wide world.

We ask this through Jesus Christ our Lord. **Amen.**

Leslie Griffiths

49   The Walls of Separation

The walls of separation
are high and thick and wide.
We cannot sneak around them
or tunnel underneath them,
for though they stand between us,
they're also built within us –

And so we want, we want to find
a peaceful way, a careful way,
step by step, brick by brick,
stone by stone,
to take them down.

Yet sometimes,
in a moment of surprise,
we hear the heart that's speaking,
and meet each other's eyes,
our fears dissolve,
and misconceptions fall,
and for a breathing space
there's no dividing wall.

The walls are strong and solid,
with hard and heavy stones –
the strangeness of the stranger
and memories of danger,
the terror of invasion,
the fear of losing freedom –

And so we need, we really need
a listening way, a lasting way,
step by step, brick by brick,
stone by stone,
to take them down.

So though our song is ending
and many walls remain,
we hope this loving greeting,
with every honest meeting,
each good negotiation,
each little celebration,

can give us all, for good and all,
a peaceful way, a lasting way,
step by step, brick by brick,
stone by stone,
to take them down.

Brian Wren

50 Ireland

Derry.
Londonderry.
The name you use betrays your clan.
Defensive Protestants filled with a fear that things will change
And Catholics nursing bitter anger over ancient wrongs.
Loyalty to crown and faith, that's one group's stance;
Dispossession, exploitation, persecution, the experience of the other.

Above and beyond the walls of this city,
Walls where apprentice boys march,
Streets where confrontation looms,
Above the Bogside
And the memorial to the dead of Bloody Sunday,–
That running sore, that unhealed wound,
Those unanswered questions,
A towering indictment of the way things have been,–
Yes, above the Bogside, and beyond the city walls,
You see the vast and rising Creggan estate,
Bleak and rambling, full of old resentments.
You can feel the alienation, the oppression,
The tangible air of a people's deepest sadness;
And you wonder when, how, whether
Such utter dejection
Such polarised opposition
Will ever be done with, over and done with, dealt with, gone.

Can the arms stretched out on a cross, you wonder,
The arms of a Jesus both camps honour
Spread far enough, wide enough to embrace all these suffering people
With his undifferentiated, undistinguishing love?

But wait! This Creggan hill was in the mind and before the eyes
Of Fanny Alexander when she wrote her hymn,
The one we sing with gusto every year in Holy Week;

> *There is a green hill far away*
> *Outside a city wall,*
> *Where the dear Lord was crucified*
> *Who died to save us all.*

Londonderry not Jerusalem inspired these words.
And she knew he'd died for Derry too.
And that's her answer to all the things we long for,
Yearn for, pray for, work for, hope for
Against the odds of reason and experience.

Capture us, dear Lord, with the power, the saving, suffering love of Jesus,
and fire us to make real the healing benefits of his cross in our own day.

Leslie Griffiths

May the strength of God pilot us.
May the power of God preserve us.
May the wisdom of God instruct us.
May the hand of God protect us.
May the way of God direct us.
May the shield of God defend us.
May the host of God guard us
    against the snares of the evil one
    and the temptations of the world.
May Christ be with us
Christ above us
Christ in us
Christ before us.
May your salvation, O Lord, be always ours
This day and for evermore.

Prayer of St Patrick

Lord Jesus Christ,
You are the way of peace.
Come into the brokenness of this land
With your healing love.
Help us to be willing to bow before you
In true repentence
And to bow to one another
In real forgiveness.
By the fire of your Holy Spirit
Melt our hard hearts and consume
The pride and prejudice
Which separate us from each other.
Fill us, O Lord, with your perfect love
Which casts out fear
And binds us together in that unity
Which you share with the father
And the Holy Spirit forever. **Amen.**

A Prayer for Continued Peace in Ireland

Our Father,
who art in Heaven,
hallowed be thy name.
Thy Kingdom come.
Thy will be done,
on earth as it is in Heaven.
Give us this day our daily bread.
And forgive our trespasses,
as we have forgiven those who trespass against us.
For if we haven't, there isn't much point going any further.
But, if we have, then we dare ask for two great favours:
to be delivered from all evil and to learn to live together in peace.
Go naofar D'aninm.
For thine is the Kingdom, the Power and the Glory,
for ever and ever.
Amen.

35

51 In this world of violence, Lord

SANCTION (7.6.10 10.6.)

David McCarthy (1931–)

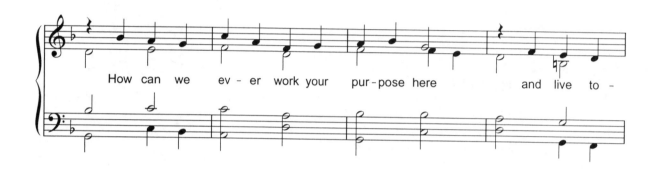

Words and Music © 1991 Stainer & Bell Ltd

1 In this world of violence, Lord,
   how can we speak your word?
   How can we ever work your purpose here
   and live together, free at last from fear?
   How can we speak your word?

2 There is violence everywhere,
   more than our thoughts can bear:
   spirits are broken, bodies crushed and bruised,
   minds robbed of knowledge, dignity refused;
   and people in despair.

3 In confusion, torn apart,
   condemned before we start:
   we meet within the hatred that we see,
   within the violence and the tyranny,
   the guilt of our own heart.

4 Here, before the cross we stand
   and Christ gives his command:
   'Love one another' – easy words to hear,
   but hard to live by in the grip of fear:
   we dare not understand.

5 Weak and by the cross deterred,
   help us at all times, Lord
   – engaged by love to take the risk of loss,
   condemned to join the fight or bear the cross –
   somehow to speak your word.

   Alan Gaunt

52   The Mostar Bridge

Grace and elegance much more than rock and mortar
Seemed its main materials;
Suleyman's jewel, little wonder of the world,
Spanned the Neretva river with so little effort.
Gasps of awe it drew across the centuries,
Wonder at the simple beauty of the thing.

What took nine years to build
Needed a mere nine days to destroy.
And the miracle of Mostar is no more.

Orthodox Serbs ousted Catholic Croats and their Muslim neighbours
With guns and bombs
Before Croats and Muslims rose up and turned the tide,
To force a Serb withdrawal.
And then the Croats turned on Muslim neighbours
Cleansing Mostar of their presence.

The bridge across Neretva stands in ruins now.
But other bridges too have been destroyed;
The bridge of trust that held communities together,
The bridge of love which linked all those of different faith,
Have been demolished with wanton heartlessness.

A new sleek bridge, all shining aluminium, leaps today across the gorge.
From its slender crossing can be seen the lost magnificence
Of the old majestic Mostar bridge
Which appears up-river like an accusing ghost
Etched into white rock.

The deep chasms of broken trust,
The swirling waters of lurking suspicion,
The fathomless abyss of division and hatred,
These need bridging now.

God help the people of Bosnia-Herzegovina.
Heal their wounds, restore their life.
Where there is doubt bring faith,
Where there is despair, hope,
Where there is hatred, love.
Build a brand new bridge, O Lord,

With faith and hope and love its main materials.
And if it takes nine days, nine years, to build it Lord,
So be it.
But let it last for ever.

Leslie Griffiths

53 Albania

We pray for a country imploding before our eyes.
And for its people who've known every form of subjection and oppression
and who now face the dictatorship of confusion, the tyranny of the unknown.

O Lord, show thy mercy upon this thy people,
And grant them thy salvation.

We pray for a country whose centuries of feudalism ended with defeat at the hands of the Ottoman Empire; and which, when the Turks finally left, enjoyed a short-lived time of independence before being occupied by Mussolini's Italy. And who, after the Fascists had gone, saw the Communists take their place and impose the bleakest, the most chilling, paranoid and oppressive time of them all, with God cast into outer darkness.

O Lord, guide the rulers of Albania,
And mercifully hear them when they call upon thee.

We give thanks for the religious leaders of Albania, rejoicing at the wholesome trust that exists between Moslems and Christians of the Roman Catholic and Orthodox traditions.

Endue thy ministers with righteousness,
And make thy chosen people joyful.

We pray for a land whose clearest symbol in recent times has been that offered by children armed with looted Kalashnikovs and hand grenades.

O Lord, save thy people,
And bless thine inheritance.

We read with horror of the way evil spirits are rushing to fill the power vacuum left by the demise of communism:
- Capitalist fraudsters with their pyramid investment schemes that have robbed so many people of their life savings;
- the Mafia barons sensing a safe haven for their drug dealing networks;
- opportunist politicians with an eye for power but little to offer.

Give peace in our time, O Lord;
Because there is none other that fighteth for us, but only thou O God.

And finally we pray for the communities where social disruption in Albania may well have serious repercussions, especially the Albanian population of Kosovo which stretches into parts of Serbia, Macedonia and Greece.

O God, hold fast this people which thou hast made in thine own image,
And take not thy Holy Spirit from them.

O God, from whom all holy desires, all good counsels, and all just works do proceed; Give unto thy servants that peace which the world cannot give; that both their hearts may be set to obey thy commandments, and also that by thee they being defended from the fear of their enemies, may pass their time in rest and quietness, through the merits of Jesus Christ our Saviour. **Amen.**

Leslie Griffiths

54 Bulgaria

Burgas, Plovdiv, Sofia: who knows about these places? who cares?
The last of the Communist dominoes to fall.
Another stretcher case for the IMF.
Squeezed between the Serbian devil and the deep Black Sea.
Vital for the stability of the Balkans.
Important to the oil-rich nations to the south-east.
Bulgaria.

Its known associations are not inspiring.
Home to a dualistic heresy that tore Christendom to pieces;
a swear-word is one of its most familiar exports.
Is that really all? What about the church?

The church created modern Bulgaria a century ago.
It fiercely opposed Nazi plans to deport Jews to the camps.
But it also offered uncritical support to Marxist governments.
Its priests now fight publicly on the steps of Alexandur Nevsky cathedral in Sofia
as factions fight for control of the church.
Schism, disarray and despair have disabled the church from playing the role of
midwife to the new Bulgaria waiting to be born.

Burgas, Plovdiv, Sofia: who wants to know about these places? or care?

God knows.
God cares.

Hasten, O Lord, the day when the Bulgarian people can enjoy freedom,
security, justice and peace.

Grant her leaders, temporal and spiritual, the wisdom, courage and humility
they require in this hour of their people's greatest need.

Through Jesus Christ our Lord. **Amen.**

Leslie Griffiths

55 Hostages

Loving and caring God,

Hear us as we pray for those who've been taken hostage.
If they linger in solitary confinement, give them a sense of your presence.
If they look down the barrel of a gun, give them a sense of your peace.
Strengthen those who love them, long for news of them, yearn for their release.
And keep them in our hearts and minds long after the newspapers have given up interest in them.
This we ask in the name of our Lord Jesus Christ, friend of the friendless and lover of us all.
Amen.

Leslie Griffiths

56   Writers in Prison

They write and what they write strikes home.
Dictators tremble at their words and quake with fearsome anger and throw them into prison.

Their spirit isn't crushed, the urge to write remains, the ode goes on;
sharply focused images hammered out on the anvil of bitter experience,
minds roaming free, mocking the restrictions which cage their bodies.
They are frontline troops, their swords beaten into penknibs,
a fighting battalion in the war against tyranny all over the world.
    – Arthur Koestler in Spain,
    – Irina Ratushinskaya and Alexander Solzhenitsyn in the old USSR,
    – Jacobo Timerman in Argentina,
    – Nien Chang in China,
    – Albie Sachs in South Africa,
    – Yannis Ritsos in Greece,
    – and countless others incarcerated in some dark dungeon's earless den.

"Prison is man-made and manned by man," one wrote. "That's why, since men are negligent,
corrupt and lazy, it's been possible to think of survival. And it *is* survival," he continues,
"survival not hope, that matters. Hope is what you need least in prison. A lump of sugar would
be more useful."

Angel Cuadra, at one point in his fifteen year spell in a Cuban jail, wrote:

> *I am only the outline of a poem*
> *between iron bars and shadow,*
> *a voice that they've tried to strangle*
> *with mutes.*

God bless all prisoners of conscience,
and especially those who are poets and writers.
May their voices always be raised in the cause of freedom.
Let suffering never stifle what they burn to say.
May their words destroy the bastions of power defended by dictators, tyrants and despots.
And may they be granted unquenchable courage in their time of pain and deprivation.
May they count on the persistence of our prayer and our undying gratitude.

Leslie Griffiths

57   A Prayer of Alexander Solzhenitsyn

How easy, Lord, it is for me to live with you.
How easy it is for me to believe in you.
When my understanding is perplexed by doubts
or on the point of giving up,
when the most intelligent men see no further
than the coming evening, and know not
what they shall do tomorrow,
you send me a clear assurance
that you are there and that you will ensure
that not all the roads of goodness are barred.

From the heights of earthly fame I look back
in wonder at the road that led
through hopelessness
to this place whence I can send
mankind a reflection of your radiance.

And whatever I in this life may yet reflect,
that you will give me;
And whatever I shall not attain,
that, plainly, you have purposed for others.

Alexander Solzhenitsyn

58 Plight of the asylum seeker

He stood before the court in nondescript clothes,
no papers, no fixed address.
The judge cleared his throat,
"Have you anything to say
before I pass sentence?"
What might have been his answer
had the prisoner the gift of speech
and the court the gift of hearing?

"I am condemned because your law
allows no place for me.
My crimes I freely admit:–
I am homeless, seeking shelter
where I may rear my family in modest decency.
I am stateless, seeking a country
where I may belong by right in God's good earth.
I am destitute, claiming a share of the wealth
that is our common heritage.
I am a sinner, needing aid from fellow sinners.

"You will dispose of me according to your law,
but you will not so easily dispose of him
who owns me citizen in his kingdom.
He frowns on crimes your law condones;
pride, selfishness and greed,
self-righteousness,
the worship of all things material
and the refusal to acknowledge me as brother.

"By your law I stand condemned;
but one day you must answer
to the master of us all
for the havoc caused by your law
in his realm."

Edmund Banyard

59 Psalm 88

Lord, my God, by day I call for help,
by night I cry aloud in your presence.
Let my prayers come before you,
hear my loud entreaty;
for I have had my fill of woes,
which have brought me to the brink of Sheol.
I am numbered with those who go down to the
    abyss;
I have become like a man beyond help,
abandoned among the dead,
like the slain lying in the grave
whom you hold in mind no more,
who are cut off from your care.
You have plunged me into the lowest abyss,
into the darkest regions of the depths.
Your wrath bears heavily on me,
you have brought on me all your fury.
You have removed my friends far from me
and made me utterly loathsome to them.
I am shut in with no escape;
my eyes are dim with anguish.
Lord, every day I have called to you
and stretched out my hands in prayer.

Will it be for the dead you work wonders?
Or can the shades rise up and praise you?
Will they speak in the grave of your love,
of your faithfulness in the tomb?
Will your wonders be known in the region of
    darkness,
your victories in the land of oblivion?

Revised English Bible

60 Lock up all the Prophets

LOCK UP ALL THE PROPHETS

Philip Banyard (fl. 1973)

Lock up all the pro-phets, si-lence the wise men, root out all the saints for the
U – ni-ty in all things is our one sal – va – tion; a – ny one who dif – fers is

state is all.
head – ing for a fall. Yet the word it is a – live

and the word it will be heard, for a man's on – ly mor – tal, though

he shakes the na – tions, he must hear the liv–ing word.

1 Lock up all the prophets,
   silence the wise men,
   root out all the saints
   for the state is all.
   Unity in all things
   is our one salvation;
   anyone who differs
   is heading for a fall.
   Yet the word it is alive
   and the word it will be heard,
   for a man's only mortal, though he shakes the nations,
   he must hear the living word.

2 Discipline the students,
   sack the professors,
   crush the dissidents
   for the state is all.
   Unity in all things
   is our one salvation;
   and anyone who differs
   is heading for a fall.
   Chorus

3 Persecute the artists,
   censor the writers,
   stop anything original,
   the state is all.
   Unity in all things
   is our one salvation;
   and anyone who differs
   is heading for a fall.
   Chorus

Philip Banyard

43

61 Martin Luther King

A Memorial Prayer offered in the Chapel of Duke University, April 9th 1968.

O God of all peoples and races and nations,
We thank you for the life of your servant Martin Luther King Jr,
    the joy and freedom of his song,
    the depth and range of his compassion,
    the faith and fervour of his prayer,
    the discipline and devotion of his mind,
    the glow and eloquence of his word,
    the courage and persistence of his march,
    the power of his inclusive love, his non-violent action,
        his trust in the eventual response of others,
        his trust in you.

We thank you for
his fearless exposure of wrongs,
    his clarion call for their righting,
    his challenging word to our consciences,
    his effective power in political action,
    his faithful witness against all war,
    his willingness to give his life for his people,
        for all people, for you.

We confess
    our own involvement in his great tragedy,
    our hardness of heart,
    our slowness to act,
    our blindness to the sufferings and injustices of those around us,
    our own deep-set racism, prejudice, discrimination,
    our complicity in decades of privileged profiting from the sufferings
        of others,
    our resistance to the cost of righting the inequities of our society,
        of our community,

You know, O God, how cheaply we take the sacrifice of this your servant, how glibly we talk and how miserably we fail. O God our God, high and lofty one, have mercy on us, forgive us our sin, grant us your peace.

We thank you now for the opportunities you go on giving us to be awakened and directed, and committed to responsible service and we pray that we may have the courage to grasp those opportunities and become instruments of your grace, agents for the transforming of society, ready to bear the cost of witnessing to your justice and your love.

Through Jesus Christ our Lord.
Amen.

McMurray S. Richey

62 Build me a Son, O Lord

General Douglas MacArthur wrote this prayer to his son in the Philippines during the early days of the Pacific War. The family included this credo many times in their morning devotions.

Build me a son, O Lord,
    who will be strong enough to know when he is weak,
    and brave enough to face himself when he is afraid;
    one who will be proud and unbending in honest defeat,
    and humble and gentle in victory.

Build me a son, O Lord,
    whose wishes will not take the place of deeds;
    a son who will know Thee
    and that to know himself is the foundation stone of knowledge.

Lead him, I pray,
    not in the path of ease and comfort,
    but under the stress and spur of difficulties and challenge.
    Here let him learn to stand up in the storm;
    here let him learn compassion for those who fail.

Build me a son, O Lord,
    whose heart will be clear,
    whose goal will be high;
    a son who will master himself before he seeks to master others,
    one who will reach into the future,
    yet never forget the past.

And after these things are his, add, I pray
    enough of a sense of humour so that
    he may always be serious yet never take himself too seriously.

Give him humility, so that
    he may always remember the simplicity of true greatness;
    the open mind of true wisdom,
    and the meekness of true strength.

Then I, his father, will dare to whisper, "I have not lived in vain."

Douglas MacArthur

63 Where is God?

These lines were written after reading *Shadows of Auschwitz: a Christian response to the Holocaust* by Harry James Cargas.

I look at the photographs
In silence
Deep, deep silence.
One question rises
Imperiously;
Where is God?

Bodies are carted into
The inextinguishable blaze
Of gaping ovens;
Human bones piled in little hills
Waiting to be turned into fertilizer
Macabre transubstantiation;
Where is God?

Three corpses hang limply from a gibbet
Swollen tongues loll heavily
A soldier poses for a snapshot
Beneath this grim calvary
Proud, it seems, of his part
In blasphemy;
Where is God?

Cadavers strewn at random
In a common grave
Big as a football field;
Featureless bodies who
Once were men and women
Boys and girls
Made for life and love;
Where is God?

Human hair made into rugs
Flesh turned into soap
Skin into lampstands
Gold fillings extracted
Melted down
Nothing wasted;
Nothing lost;
Where is God?

In a world like this
Where is God?
In the world you made
Where are you God?

Leslie Griffiths

64 Words of Dag Hammarskjöld

You dare your Yes – and experience a meaning.
You repeat your Yes – and all things acquire a meaning.
When everything has a meaning, how can you live anything
    but a Yes?

Dag Hammarskjöld

65 A Prayer by a South African Jew

Let the healing grace of your love, oh Lord, so transform me that I may play my part in the transfiguration of the world from a place of suffering, death and corruption to a realm of infinite light, joy and love. Make me so obedient to your spirit that my life may become a living prayer and a witness to your unfailing presence.

Martin Israel

66 Words found in the Warsaw ghetto

I believe in the sun even when it does not shine,
I believe in love, even when I cannot feel it.
I believe in God, even when I do not see him.

Inscribed on the walls of a building in the Warsaw ghetto

67 A New Rabbi's Prayer

Extracts from a speech made by Rabbi Tirzah ben-David on the day of her ordination in July 1996 at the West London Synagogue.

"See, I come carrying a book, telling the story of my life."

These are the words of the Psalmist.

So many of you, of course, are in that book; you helped to write it. Your names are on the pages, and your fingerprints, and the odd blotch and tearstain: and some who should be here are missing, and there's an empty space where they ought to be.

It's been a long and somewhat rambling history up to now; but this new chapter has a grand and rather frightening title: "Tirzah ben-David, Rabbi and Teacher in Israel." And I try to imagine all the people, both known and unknown, who are going to help me to write it. Every new beginning needs a prayer. I offer this one on behalf of everyone who hears their own voice in it somewhere:

> *Dear God, guard my doubts and my uncertainties,*
> *Their going out and their coming in:*
> *And bless all those blessed questions that keep me*
> *knocking at your door.*
>
> *I don't know if I am worthy*
> *But I want to be worthwhile.*
>
> *The spirit hovers, breathless,*
> *Waiting for the light:*
> *Is this the way it always feels, Lord,*
> *On the first day?*

Rabbi Tirzah ben-David

68 Gypsies

People with nowhere left to go;
reviled, hated, persecuted.
Romanies, migrants from India,
roaming, fleeing, travelling, always on the move.
Six million: two words that still draw breath,
a figure that's become a metaphor for
man's utter depravity, his inhumanity to man.
But who remembers the half million gypsies
who endured the same concentration camps,
      suffered the same medical experimentation,
      underwent the same forcible sterilisation programme
as did the Jews?

"Cursed is the land from which gypsies flee:"
runs an old Serb proverb to remind us of how things are.
We mustn't forget. *Zakhor.* Remember.

O God, help us to be more tolerant of gypsies;
to cherish their culture and learn from their way of life.
Save us from stereotyping, stigmatising, scapegoating them.
Open our eyes to see this travelling, wandering race
    as indeed the people of God.

Through Jesus Christ our Lord, who himself had no fixed abode, and who with you and the Holy Spirit lives and reigns, one God now and forever. **Amen.**

Leslie Griffiths

69 The Tambourine Woman

WEAVING (9.8.9.8.D. Anapaestic & Refrain)

June Boyce-Tillman (1943–)

With a dance lilt

One day as I went out a-walk-ing, a stran-ger ap-peared un-to me. Her
skirt was made up of weird pat-ches, a rain-bow in bold ta-pes-try. Silk
rib-bons be-gui-ling in co-lour flowed out from her strange tam-bou-rine. Behind her a vast crowd of peo-ple came leap-ing and sing-ing this theme: *We'll*
fol-low the tam-bou-rine wo-man and join in her tam-bou-rine song. We're
ri-ding a rain-bow to hea-ven and dan-cing our jour-ney a-long.

1 One day as I went out a-walking,
   a stranger appeared unto me.
   Her skirt was made up of weird patches,
   a rainbow in bold tapestry.
   Silk ribbons beguiling in colour
   flowed out from her strange tambourine.
   Behind her a vast crowd of people
   came leaping and singing this theme:
   We'll follow the tambourine woman
   and join in her tambourine song.
   We're riding a rainbow to heaven
   and dancing our journey along.

2 She showed me at first yellow patches,
   the colour of newness and spring,
   of daffodils, lemon and honey,
   the freshness a new birth can bring.
   But next to them lay the deep purples
   or mourning, of sadness, of grief,
   of velvet and softness and richness,
   of heathers on moorland and heath.
   Chorus

3 The diamond patches were orange
   as rays in the heart of the sun,
   vibrating with warmth and with loving
   and speaking of victories won.
   But scattered around them were brown ones
   that spoke of the healing of earth,
   a gentleness, depth and enfolding,
   the loving that knows its own worth.
   Chorus

4 The reds spoke of magic and anger,
   enchantment, bewitchment and spells,
   of fire that flickers and sparkles,
   but also of judgment and hells.
   The blues and the greens were much softer
   and blended to form a deep lake.
   Unfathomable she described it;
   we felt we would drown for her sake.
   Chorus

5 The song grew in depth and wideness
   and plaited a curious weave
   of colourful tambourine ribbons,
   so none of us wanted to leave.
   We found we reflected her colours
   and singing was making them one –
   our tapestry vibrant with colour
   and woven with laughter and fun.
   Chorus

June Boyce-Tillman

70 The Weaver

When I climb to the old weaver's house,
I watch, astonished at all that spills forth
    from her mind:
a thousand designs taking shape
and no model to copy
the marvellous fabric
with which she will clothe
the Companion of the Faithful and True One.

Men always ask me
to give them the brand name
or show them patterns.
But the Weaver will not be boxed in
by formulas or patterns.
All her fabrics are originals
and none are repeat models.
Her mind races beyond all foresight.
Her able hands accept no patterns or models:
What will appear will appear,
but She Who is will make it.

The colours of her thread are strong:
blood, sweat, perseverance, tears,
    struggle and hope.
Colours that do not fade with time.
The children of the children of our own children
will recognize the stamp of the Old Weaver.
Perhaps then her work will be given a name.
But the model can never again be repeated.

I have seen how each morning her able fingers
select the threads one by one.

Her loom makes no noise
and we pay little attention to her,
yet still
the design that comes forth from Her Mind
hour after hour
will appear in the threads of many colours
in figures and symbols
that no one ever again
will be able to erase or undo.

Julia Esquival, Guatemalan Theologian

71 Prayer of the Incas in search of God

Hear me,
from the sky above
where you stay,
from the sea below where you are.
Creator of the world,
potter,
Lord of Lords,
my eyes long to see you,
I long to know you;
knowing you,
thinking of you,
understanding you,
you will see me and will know me.

The sun, the moon,
the day,
the night,
the summer,
the winter,
do not walk in vain;
they are orderly,
and walk to the determined place
and arrive successfully.

Everywhere you go
you carry with you
your king's sceptre.
Hear me,
listen to me.
Lest I tire,
lest I die.

Eduardo Galeano, Memoria del Fuego

72 What is sin? a Buddhist monk replies

A Buddhist monk was once asked: "What is sin?" Very often in the East, a question is answered by a question, it is part of their wisdom, a result of deep meditation. The monk asked the pupil to spread his hands wide open. "What can you do with our open hands?" The reply was: "I can arrange flowers, embrace a loved one, work and in general do all manner of things." All beautiful things he thought to himself. Then the monk went on: "Now, close your hands slowly, till they're tightly closed. What have you now? What can you do with your hands like this?"

The pupil did as he was told and stared at his two fists. He realised the terrible things he could do with his hands like this and finally he said: "I can hurt, injure, even kill someone." "That," said the monk, "is what sin is."

From The Tablet

73 Buddhism

Vietnamese Buddhist monk, Thich Nhat Hanh, writes of the need for heightened awareness to discover the essential reality at the heart of everything.

Life has left her footprints on my forehead
but I have become a child again this morning.
The smile, seen through leaves and flowers, is back, to smooth
away the wrinkles
As the rains wipe away footprints on the beach. Again a
cycle of birth and death begins.

I walk on thorns, but firmly, as among flowers.
I keep my head high.
Rhymes bloom among the sounds of bombs and mortars.
The tears I shed yesterday have become rain,
I feel calm hearing its sound on the thatched roof.
Childhood (O my birthland!) is calling me
And the rain melts my despair.

I am still alive, able to smile quietly. The sweet fruit
brought forth by the tree of sufferings!
Carrying the dead body of my brother, I go across the rice-field
in the darkness.
Earth will keep thee tight within her arms, dear one,
so that tomorrow thou wilt be reincarnated in flowers—
those flowers smiling quietly in the morning field.
This moment you weep no more, dear one— we have gone through
too deep a night!

This morning, yes, this morning, I kneel down on the green grass
when I feel your presence.
O flowers which sing to me in silence!
The message,
the message of love and sacrifice
has indeed come to us.

Thich Nhat Hanh

Heightened awareness is not only the key that unlocks the secrets of the material world, it also opens the way to a mystical understanding of God's own self and God's own way for us. As Charles Wesley knew too well:

Open, Lord, my inward ear,
　　And bid my heart rejoice;
Bid my quiet spirit hear
　　Thy comfortable voice;
Never in the whirlwind found,
　　Or where earthquakes rock the place,
Still and silent is the sound,
　　The whisper of thy grace.

Lord, my time is in thy hand,
　　My soul to thee convert;
Thou canst make me understand,
　　Though I am slow of heart;
Thine in whom I live and move,
　　Thine the work, the praise is thine;
Thou art wisdom, power, and love,
　　And all thou art is mine.

Charles Wesley

74 Pilgrims' Hymn for Peace, Truth and Unity

PILGRIMS' HYMN

Donald Swann (1923–1994)

Moderato ♩ = 120

We ask that we live and we la-bour in peace, in peace. Each

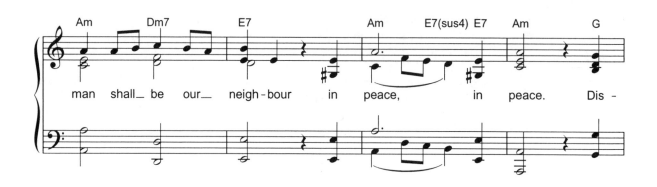

man shall_ be our_ neigh-bour in peace, in peace. Dis -

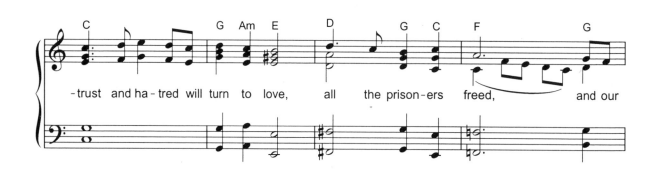

-trust and ha-tred will turn to love, all the prison-ers freed, and our

on - ly war will be the one a-gainst all hu - man need.

1 We ask that we live and we labour in peace, in peace.
Each man shall be our neighbour in peace, in peace.
Distrust and hatred will turn to love,
all the prisoners freed,
and our only war will be the one
against all human need.

2 We work for the end of disunion in truth, in truth.
That all may be one communion in truth, in truth.
We choose the road of peace and prayer
countless pilgrims trod,
so that Hindu, Moslem, Christian, Jew
we all can worship one God.

3 We call to our sisters and brothers, unite, unite!
That all may live for others, unite, unite!
And so the nations will be as one,
one the flag unfurled,
one law, one faith, one hope, one truth,
one people and one world.

Donald Swann

75 Aboriginal Prayer

Read in Westminster Abbey, 20 April 1997

God of holy dreaming, Great Creator Spirit,
from the dawn of creation you have given your children
the good things of Mother Earth.
You spoke and the gum tree grew.
In the vast desert and dense forest,
and in cities at the water's edge,
creation sings your praise.
Your presence endures
as the rock at the heart of our Land.
When Jesus hung on the tree
you heard the cries of all your people
and became one with your wounded ones:
the convicts, the hunted and the dispossessed.
The sunrise of your Son coloured the earth anew,
and bathed it in glorious hope.
In Jesus we have been reconciled to you,
to each other and to your whole creation.
Lead us on, Great Spirit,
as we gather from the four corners of the earth;
enable us to walk together in trust
from the hurt and shame of the past
into the full day which has dawned in Jesus Christ. **Amen.**

From A Prayer Book for Australia

76 Shinto

Shinto has no clearcut theology,
     no idea of a single unique Supreme Being.
But it has a definite sense of the numinous which is to be found in:
     – the warmth of the sun;
     – the miracle of clear running streams;
     – the life force of the winds;
     – the strength of great rocks.
Shinto has never felt attracted to a Christian God who has been put forward as
     – masculine;
     – cold and forbidding;
     – harsh.

We pray for grace to stand with Shinto in rediscovering the sense of God's presence within the created order;

and to learn from Shinto how to present our God in warmer, softer, more intuitive ways.

Let our Christian discipleship be painted always in the colours of wonder, love, and praise.

Through Jesus Christ our Lord. **Amen.**

Leslie Griffiths

77 A Masai Prayer

Creator God
we announce your goodness because
it is clearly visible in the heavens
where there is the light of the sun,
the heat of the sun,
and the light of night
and the rain clouds.

Your love is visible all the time:
morning and daytime, evening and night.
Your love is great.
It has filled the land; it has filled the people.

We say "Thank you, our God" because you have
given us everything we have.
You have given us our mothers and fathers,
our sisters and brothers,
our children and friends.
You are our shield; you protect us.
You are our guard; you take care of us.
You are our safety, all our days.
You stay with us for ever and ever.

We worship you with our mouths.
We worship you with our bodies.
We worship you with everything we have,
because it is you who has given us everything we have.

We say "Thank you" today,
and tomorrow, and all our days.
We do not tire of giving thanks to you
for your love and faithfulness.

Leslie Griffiths

78 India

And if you would know God,
Be not therefore a solver of riddles.
Rather look around you and you shall see him
Playing with your children.

Kahlil Gibran

79 Sweden

Thou takest the pen – and the lines dance;
Thou takest the flute – and the notes shimmer;
Thou takest the brush – and the colours sing.
So all things have meaning and beauty
in the space and time where thou art.
How then can I hold anything back from thee?

Dag Hammarskjöld

80 Latin America

I had a paint box
but it didn't have the colour red
for the blood of the wounded,
nor white
for the hearts and faces of the dead.

It didn't have yellow either
for the burning sands
of the desert.

Instead it had orange
for the dawn and the sunset
and blue
for new skies
and pink
for the dreams of young people.

I sat down and painted peace.

A Child of 10

81 Malaysia

Portrait of an old lady

A lifetime of shuttling
to and from rooms
the size of handkerchiefs.

Fetching and carrying
cooking and scrubbing
shaping the ramshackle

kiosk into a habitable
home for her children
her children's children.

Never complaining, but
time exacted its toll:
that weight of years

stooped her shoulders
and decades of pinched air
imploded her

dry weather-polished
face into a diaspora
of pain-scorched rivers.

Cecil Rajendra

82 Philippines

From the author's book *How Long? Prison Reflections*

Beyond the darkness, there is light.
Beyond the griefs and pains of the moment
is the promise of food and freedom for all.

Beyond our current distress is the dream
of a tapestry through which is woven
the rainbow colours of truth, freedom,
peace and love. And in the centre of
this tapestry is the Son of God who
became human to uphold the Kingdom
of justice and righteousness.

Karl Gaspar

83 Freedom

Rising in the morn I cry
"Come freedom today!"
At mid-day I sit and sigh,
"When comes the great day?"
God! to thee I bring my sorrow,
Tears I daily weep;
Must they be my tomorrow?
If so, give me sleep.

W. M. B. Nhlapo, 1950

84 The Gandhi Talisman

Recall the face of the poorest and
most helpless person whom you may
have seen and ask yourself
if the step you contemplate is
going to be of any use to him;
will he be able to gain anything by it?
Will it restore him to control
over his life and destiny?

M. K. Gandhi

85 Show me the Way

Grant that I may so
Thy steps track here below,
That in the masques and shadows I may see
Thy sacred way
And by those hid ascents climb to that day
which breaks from thee
who art in all things, though invisibly;
show me thy peace,
thy mercy, love and ease.

Henry Vaughan

86 An Indian Medical Student's Paraphrase of 1 Corinthians 13

If I have language ever so perfectly and speak like a pundit and have not the knack of love that grips the heart,

I am nothing.

If I have decorations and diplomas, and am proficient in up-to-date methods, and have not the touch of understanding love,

I am nothing.

If I am able to worst my opponents in arguments so as to make fools of them, and have not the wooing note,

I am nothing.

If I have all faith and great ideals and magnificent plans and wonderful visions, and have not the love that sweats and bleeds and weeps and prays and pleads,

I am nothing.

If I surrrender all prospects and, leaving home and friends and comforts, give myself to the self-evident sacrifice of a missionary career, and turn sour and selfish amid the daily annoyances and personal slights of a missionary life, and though I give my body to be consumed in the heat and sweat and mildew of India, if I have not the love that yields its rights, its coveted leisure, its pet plans,

I am nothing, nothing.

Virtue has ceased to go out of me.

If I can heal all manner of sickness and disease, but wound hearts and hurt feeling for want of love that is kind,

I am nothing.

If I can write books and publish articles that set the world agog, and fail to transcribe the word of the Cross in the language of love,

I am nothing.

An Indian Medical Student

87 Russia

Holy Russia, third Rome, land of saints and mystics, has also been home to the gulag and militant atheism. At its heart has been a struggle for identity between old Slavic voices and those who look towards the rationalism of Europe. It is the land whose most recognizable symbols are the icon and the axe. What follows is a description of the origins of Christianity in Russia:

> The darkness of the demonic cult perished and the sun of the Gospel shone over our land. The temples of idols were destroyed, and the churches were built, the idols were broken and the icons of the saints appeared. Demons fled away, the cross sanctified the towns; as shepherds of spiritual lambs, came bishops, priests and deacons, offering the immaculate sacrifice. They adorned all the sanctuary and vested holy churches with beauty. Angel's trumpet and Gospel's thunder sounded through all the towns. The incense rising towards God sanctified the air. Monasteries stood on mountains. Men and women, small and great, all people filled holy churches.
>
> [*Hilarion, Archbishop of Kiev, 11th Century*]

According to philosopher Nikolai Berdyaev (1874–1948) in his *Spirits of the Russian Revolution*, Russian thought has been apocalyptic as its "positive pole" and nihilistic at its "negative pole." The French character is in tension between dogmatism and scepticism, the German between mysticism and criticism. Russian self-consciousness, however,

> is not interested in any cultural values, but strives towards an end, a frontier... In the Russian sectarians, apocalypticism is interwoven and mixed with nihilism. The same is true of the Russian intelligensia. The Russian search for the truth in life always takes on an apocalyptic or a nihilistic character... This prepares the ground for all kinds of confusions and delusions, for pseudo-religions... Even Russian atheism has pseudo-religious features, a kind of religion in reverse... A culture can be founded on dogmatism and scepticism, mysticism and criticism. But it is difficult, extremely difficult, to found a culture on apocalypticism and nihilism. A culture can have dogmatic and mystical depth. But it requires that some value be recognized outside the life process itself, that not just what is absolute, but also that which is relative, may be of significance.

There is a great need for a modern and viable Russian spirituality which will integrate the past. Otherwise there might be a real risk that it will sublimate itself again in a headlong totalitarianism.

Since *glasnost* and *perestroika* and the collapse of the Soviet empire, huge and often uncontrollable energies have been released from deep within the Russian psyche. People have come to understand that a schizoid and oppressive intrusiveness and disorder characterised life for most of the Russian people for most of the time during the years of communism. Everything now seems to be in a flux. As Robert Service, Professor of Russian History and Politics at the University of London School of Slavonic and East European Studies put it (*The Guardian*, October 25th 1997)

> Capitalism has hit Russia like a tornado. The welfare safety net has been torn apart, and most Russians turn to traditional structures and practices to cope with the massive dislocation of living conditions and the remorseless degradation of the economic and natural environment.

And criminals feed on the confusion. Politicians seem powerless and the future looks grim.

The "Breastplate" of St Patrick was composed for confusing times in the history of Britain. With only slight modification, it serves as a very appropriate prayer for the people and leaders of Russia.

May the strength of God pilot them.
May the power of God preserve them.
May the wisdom of God instruct them.
May the hand of God protect them.
May the way of God direct them.
May the shield of God defend them.
May the host of God guard them against the
    snares of evil and the temptations of the world.

May Christ be with them.
Christ before them.
Christ in them.
Christ over them.
May your salvation, O Lord, be always theirs
    this day and forever more.

Leslie Griffiths

The Elements

Earth

88 God in his love for us lent us this planet

God called the dry land earth; God saw that it was good.
God said, let the earth produce growing things,
    plants that bear seed,
    trees bearing fruit.
So it was. And God saw that it was good.   *[Genesis 1:9–12, REB]*

God in his love for us lent us this planet,
gave it a purpose in time and in space:
small as a spark from the fire of creation,
cradle of life and the home of our race.

The Lord fashioned the earth
and everything that grows in it,
giving breath to its people
and life to those who walk in it.
"I, the Lord, have called you with a righteous purpose."   *[Isaiah 42, REB]*

Thanks be to God for its bounty and beauty,
life that sustains us in body and mind:
plenty for all, if we learn how to share it,
riches undreamed of to fathom and find.

God said: "Fill the earth and subdue it; have dominion over everything that lives on the earth. All plants that bear seed, every three bearing fruit, shall be yours for food."   *[Genesis 1:28, REB]*

The Lord God took the man he'd made and put him in the garden of Eden to till it and to look after it.   *[Genesis 2:15, REB]*

Long have our human wars ruined its harvest;
long has earth bowed to the terror of force;
long have we wasted what others have need of,
poisoned the fountain of life at its source.

Abel tended the flock,
Cain worked the land.
In due season, Cain brought forth some of the fruits of the earth,
Abel the choicest of his flock.

The Lord was pleased with Abel's offering, much less so with Cain's.
Cain, in jealousy, attacked and murdered his brother.
The Lord said when he discovered this:
"Your brother's blood is crying out to me from the earth."

[Genesis 4:2–10, REB]

Casual despoilers, or high-priests of Mammon,
selling the future for present rewards,
careless of life and contemptuous of beauty:
bid them remember, the Earth is the Lord's.

Sing a new song to the Lord.
Let all the earth be glad, let the fields exult,
let all the trees of the forest shout for joy
before the Lord when he comes.   *[Psalm 96, REB]*

Earth is the Lord's: it is ours to enjoy it,
ours, as his stewards, to farm and defend.
From its pollution, misuse, and destruction,
good Lord, deliver us, world without end.

The verses are from the hymn by Fred Pratt Green

89 God's Grandeur

The world is charged with the grandeur of God.
It will flame out, like shining from shook foil;
It gathers to a greatness, like the ooze of oil
Crushed. Why do men then now not reck his rod?
Generations have trod, have trod, have trod;
And all is seared with trade; bleared, smeared with toil;
And wears man's smudge and shares man's smell: the soil
Is bare now, nor can foot feel, being shod.

And for all this, nature is never spent;
There lives the dearest freshness deep down things;
And though the last lights off the black West went
Oh, morning, at the brown brink eastward, springs –
Because the Holy Ghost over the bent
World broods with warm breast and with ah! bright wings.

Gerard Manley Hopkins

90 When God made the Garden of Creation

WHEN GOD MADE THE GARDEN OF CREATION

J.A. Paul Booth (1931–1995)

When God made the Gar-den of Cre-a-tion he filled it full of his Love.

When God made the Gar-den of Cre-a-tion he saw that it___was good. There's

room for you   and room for me   and room for ev - 'ry one,   for

God is a Fa-ther who loves his child-ren and gives them a place in the sun.

When God made the Gar-den of Cre-a-tion he filled it full of his Love.

1 When God made the Garden of Creation
   he filled it full of his Love.
   When God made the Garden of Creation
   he saw that it was good.
   There's room for you
   and room for me
   and room for everyone,
   for God is a Father who loves his children
   and gives them a place in the sun.
   When God made the Garden of Creation
   he filled it full of his Love.

2 When God made the Hamper of Creation
   he filled it full of his Love.
   When God made the Hamper of Creation
   he saw that it was good.
   There's food for you
   and food for me
   and food enough for all,
   but man is so greedy, so wastes God's bounty,
   that some won't get any at all.
   When God made the Garden of Creation
   he filled it full of his Love.

3 When God made the Family of Creation
   he filled it full of his Love.
   When God made the Family of Creation
   he saw that it was good.
   There's love for you
   and love for me
   and love for everyone;
   but man is so greedy, forgetting his neighbour;
   he seeks his own place in the sun.
   When God made the Family of Creation
   he filled it full of his Love.

4 When God made us Stewards of Creation
   he made us his Vision to share.
   When God made us Stewards of Creation
   our burdens he wanted to bear.
   He cares for you,
   he cares for me,
   he cares for all in need;
   for God is a Father who loves his children
   no matter what colour or creed.
   When God made us Stewards of Creation
   he gave us his Vision to share.

J. A. Paul Booth

63

Water

91   My Flowing Stream

As a deer longs for flowing streams,
so my soul longs for you
O God.
[Psalm 42:1, NRSV]

"I will pour water
on the thirsty land,
and streams
on the dry ground,"
says the Lord.
[Isaiah 44:3, NRSV]

Living water of Christ,
cleanse and purify me,
and be a spring of eternal life
welling up within me.

Let me trust in God,
"like a tree planted by water,
that sends out its roots by the stream,
and does not fear when heat comes."
[Jeremiah 17:8, RSV]

Lord, may your peaceful presence
be like a well of still, clear water
within me.

Lord, you are my lover,
my longing,
my flowing stream,
my sun,
and I am your reflection.
[Mechtild of Magdeburg, 13th Century]

Angela Ashwin

92 Rain on the earth by heaven's blessing

LUDHAM (9.8.9.8. Dactylic)   *Mervyn Horder (1910–1997)*

(♩ = 120)

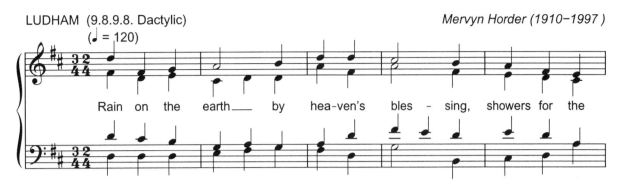

Rain on the earth___ by hea-ven's bles - sing, showers for the

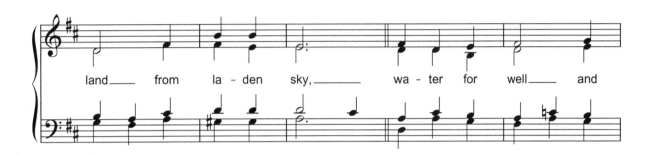

land___ from la - den sky, ___ wa - ter for well___ and

spring and ri - ver - God grant us rain,___ or else we die!___

1 Rain on the earth by heaven's blessing,
  showers for the land from laden sky,
  water for well and spring and river —
  God grant us rain, or else we die!

2 Rain is your gift for wise or wicked,
  humans and cattle, herb and tree;
  praise for its promise and its warning,
  showing your wisdom, flowing free!

3 Come to our world of drought and flooding,
  hold back their danger and their fear;
  dwell in the lands of dearth or drowning,
  help them and save them by our care.

4 Early or late, on hill and valley,
  thunderous torrent, gentle mist —
  visit in mercy, not in judgement;
  this is our prayer, who pray in Christ.

5 God send the rain to green our pastures,
  feeding our flocks, our fields and grain;
  God fill our streams in all due seasons:
  God of all grace, grant us good rain!

Christopher Idle

Wind

93 Blowing in the Wind

Wind blows through the pages of the Bible
in a surprising variety of ways.

There's the sifting wind that blows away the chaff,
 the scorching winds before whose blast everything withers,
 the silent wind that sweeps the skies clean,
 and the winds that batter, frighten, howl, lash, and beat on all we build.

It's a wind that whispers just how weak we are, how fragile and quickly passing
our moment on the stage.
 "Our human life is as grass,
 like wild flowers in the meadow;
 the wind comes and blows us all away
 and our place shows no further sign of us."

And yet the very wind which carries us away and speaks of our tenuous hold on
the thread of life becomes a metaphor to hail the mighty power of him who who
sent it.
 "Lord my God, you are very great,
 clothed in majesty and splendour,
 you take the clouds for your chariot,
 and ride on the wings of the wind."
And Jesus too evokes the same response from those around him:
 "Even the winds and waves obey him," they declare.

The winds convey something of the splendour and the otherness of God.
He makes the winds his messengers;
 he sends them freely as the waters flow;
 his Spirit, like the wind, blows where it wants to,
  you hear the sound of it but don't know where it comes from.
Like the wind, our God is a God of surprises.

And then there's Pentecost.
The Spirit came from the sky like a strong, driving wind,
 a noise that filled the whole house where the friends of Jesus were sitting.
It destroyed their resistance,
 consumed their fears,
 knocked down the barriers of their despair,
 swirled and roared into their hearts, filling their souls, changing the
direction of their lives, sweeping clean the clutter of old understandings,
empowering them to take the message out into a hostile world of apathy
and ignorance.

They were filled with the Holy Spirit sweeping into their lives.

Leslie Griffiths

94 Wind of God

Wind of God, keep on blowing,
Sail over the barriers that we build
to divide ourselves from each other.
Pick up your seeds of freedom and truth wherever they flourish,
carry them across frontiers and plant them in other soil,
to begin fresh growth and new forms.
Blow from the South
to the ears of Northern peoples.
Blow away the blinkers
which keep our eyes focused only on the past,
repeating its violence, deepening its divisions
and adding to its despair.
Reveal the new future you have in mind for us.

Speak peace where nations meet,
justice where ideas clash,
mercy where power reigns,
healing where minds and bodies hurt,
and love where churches seek your unity,
and wherever Babel drowns out the sound of Pentecost.

Graham Cook

95 We who bear the human name

We who bear the human name
are like flowers of the field;
without status, without fame,
trampled down and made to yield,
unprotected and exposed
to the scorching wind that blows.
Let all the world now blossom as a field!

Even Solomon of old
(said our Lord, the Man of peace)
with his glory and his gold
could not match the flowers' grace.
We are weak but we recall
how the mighty ones must fall.
Let all the world now blossom as a field!

We are people of the field,
crowding Asia's city streets
We are people called to build
A community of peace.
We remember as we toil
Hope is springing from the soil.
Let all the world now blossom as a field!

Fred Kaan

67

Fire

96 Inextinguishable Blaze

Raw and elemental,
burning, purging, sweeping, refining,
fire.

"Anger is like a fire burning deep within."   [Jeremiah 20:9, REB]
Lord, save me from my own consuming passions.

"God's judgement is like a fire that burns for ever."   [Isaiah 33:14, REB]
Lord, in your mercy, purge me of my wickedness and sin.

"God's message is like a fire, like a hammer that breaks."   [Jeremiah 23:29]
> **Batter my heart, three personed God; for you**
> **As yet but knock, breathe, shine, and seek to mend;**
> **That I may rise, and stand, o'erthrow me, and bend**
> **Your force, to break, blow, burn and make me new.**
>
> [John Donne, Sonnet XIV]

Fire destroys; it blazes, rages and consumes palaces, cities and forests.
Lord, sweep through my inner being like a flame of fire,
Destroy my pride, consume my prejudice, and burn away my sin.

God's own holiness is like fire; his pillar of fire guided the people through the desert;
he appeared to Moses in a bush that burned.

> **O thou who camest from above**
> **The pure celestial fire to impart,**
> **Kindle a flame of sacred love**
> **On the mean altar of my heart.**
>
> **There let it for thy glory burn**
> **With inextinguishable blaze,**
> **And trembling to its source return**
> **In humble prayer and fervent praise.**   [Charles Wesley]

And God's Spirit came, sweeping into their lives, resembling tongues of fire which
came to rest upon each of them.

> **Spirit of the living God,**
> **Fall afresh on me.**
> **Break me, melt me,**
> **Mould me, fill me.**
> **Spirit of the living God,**
> **Fall afresh on me.**   [Daniel Iverson]

Fire of God, keep on burning,
smoulder in the hearts of people
where oppression keeps them in chains.

Where unemployment and poverty devalue their humanity
and where hunger weakens the spirit;
Burn in them, like Moses' bush,
and do not let them be destroyed.

Glory be to the Father and to the Son and to the Holy Spirit,
As it was in the beginning, is now and shall be forever. Amen.

Leslie Griffiths

97 Charcoal

Dull black and dusty charcoal – useful for art and outdoor cooking – activities towards
    the leisure end of our lives.
Such unprepossessing stuff, and yet it can produce a delicately shaded drawing and
    such appetising outdoor tastes and smells.

Charcoal is far from the luxury end of the lives of other people.
It's all they have as fuel. No coal or oil; no gas or electricity.
Just lumps of the dusty black stuff.

The whiteish embers of a charcoal fire lie under steaming and simmering cauldrons in
    millions of rural homes around the world.
The slightest breeze brings forth a glow below the ashes: red breaks through the grey,
    and rice or beans or millet or corn cook merrily away while families' appetites are
    whetted.

Such an important commodity in the everyday lives of countless country people.
Tiny quantities are purchased daily; merchants arrange their wares in woefully small
    pyramids of matted, blackish lumps.
The wood that produced this fuel was once mounded under earth or turf and subjected
    to slow burning over many, many hours.
Smoke-producing organic material was burned out of it,
Higher-octane, steady-burning carbon was left for further use.

In the poorest countries of the world
The wood they turn to charcoal
Comes from trees they can't afford to be without;
Hard woods and even fruit-bearing trees,
whose cutting down strips the soil of its protection
and allows the heavy rain to carry precious earth into the distant sea,
leaving eroded hillsides and a bare tomorrow.

Strange to think that a cheerful boiling pot and the smell of the next meal,
might well announce so many dreadful woes with loss of Eden, and the inexorable
    onward march of the desert.

Leslie Griffiths

98 Like fireworks lighting up the night

SHELTERED DALE (8.6.8.6.8.6.)

German Traditional Melody

Like fire-works light - ing up the night the Ho - ly Spi - rit came:__ de - ject - ed Christ - ians felt the touch of liv - ing fronds of flame – and sud - den - ly,__ the world was young__ and no - thing looked the same.__

1 Like fireworks lighting up the night
the Holy Spirit came:
dejected Christians felt the touch
of living fronds of flame –
and suddenly, the world was young
and nothing looked the same.

2 For Jesus' nearness gave them heart
to venture, come what would:
the love of Jesus bade them share
their house, possessions, food:
the mind of Jesus gave them speech
that all men understood.

3 This is the Spirit who today
our daring will inspire
and common folk are given gifts
to change the world entire:
the sparks which flew at Pentecost
began a forest fire.

Ian Fraser

Liturgy and Reality

99 Our Father

Our Father in heaven,
remind us constantly that you are parent
to all your children, whoever and
wherever they are or come from
hallowed be your name.

Your kingdom come,
establishing peace and justice,
hope and life for all peoples,
Your will be done on earth as it is in heaven.

Give us today our daily bread,
disturb us into an awareness of the needs of others.

Forgive our sins,
our pride and also our prejudice,
As we forgive those who sin against us.

Lead us not into temptation,
especially keep our hearts and minds
open to see the good in others;
Deliver us from evil.

For the kingdom – just and true,
the power – gentle and fair,
and the glory – shot through with the colours of love,

are yours, for ever and ever. Amen.

Leslie Griffiths

100 Te Deum (1)

We the homeless praise thee O God.
We acknowledge thee to be the Lord.

Lost and alone,
Kathy come home,
struggling with kids
in Bed and Breakfast hotels
damp running down the wall,
mildew growing in our loos,
discharged from the asylum,
our marriages collapsed,
homes repossessed,
addicted to booze or drugs,
trying to forget,
cold, lonely, rejected, hopeless,
all alone is all we are.

In Hertford, Hereford and Hampshire,
hurricanes hardly ever happen.
But in the Leewards, the Philippines and Uttar Pradesh,
monsoons, tornados, cyclonic disturbance
come with frightening regularity.
They blow our houses down,
Flood waters carry them away,
stripping hillsides of whole villages,
flushing entire communities from valley bottoms,
in a single night of destruction.

And fire too wreaks its havoc;
it burns the heart out of our favella, bidonville, shanty town, slum;
it takes not only the roof from over our head,
but our little trinkets and precious possessions,
our beds and sewing machines,
the means to earn our pennies.
And yet you'll find us in the morning
sitting patiently on our haunches,
our faces impenetrable,
smiling at grief.

God shall sit every man under his vine and his fig tree
and none shall make them afraid.   [Micah 4, REB]

See, I am creating new heavens and a new earth! I am creating
Jerusalem as a delight. The sound of weeping, the cry of distress,
*will be heard in her no more. My people will build houses **and** live*
*in them, plant vineyards **and** eat their fruit; they will not build for*
others to live in or plant for others to eat. Neither hurt nor harm will
be present in that day says the Lord.   [Isaiah 65, REB]

All the earth doth worship thee;
The Father everlasting.

But, dear Lord and Father of us all,
how long must we wait for our dreams to come true?
How long, O Lord, how long?

Leslie Griffiths

101 Te Deum (2)

To thee all poor and wretched people cry aloud;
The earth and all the powerless therein.

We are wretched indeed, pariahs,
unwanted, unloved, living at the margins
of people's consciousness,
a problem, responsible for our own plight, a disgrace.

We are victims of war, famine, disaster,
trapped by economic circumstance,
pools of cheap labour boosting profits for people we never see.
We live on sink estates, messily at the edge of huge cities,
or else in isolated rural dwellings.
Structural adjustment programmes drive us further into our poverty.
Getting our children to school, enough food to eat,
access to medical care, our roof repaired,
seems harder and harder year by year.

O God, who lives in the slums, where the sewage runs
down the back of the houses;
where the mud walls crumble when the monsoon comes;
where rain soaks through the holes in roofs,
help us to know you.

O God, who crouches at church gates, where people walk by
after morning worship;
whose name is beggar, cripple, leper, pavement-dweller,
help us to know you.

O God, who lives in the outcaste street, whose children
work to clear off debt;
who hungers because you are unemployed:
who despairs because children starve and women suffer,
help us to know you.

O God, who lies down to die under the bridge in the city,
covered in a rag as the traffic roars by,
whose body is carted away by the municipal sweepers
because all have forsaken you,
help us to know you.

O God, slum-dweller, beggar, cripple, leper;
O God, without work, hungry, thirsty;
O God, forsaken, alone;
help us to know you.   *[Timothy J. Mark]*

To thee the poor and wretched of the earth
Continually do cry.

We know that Jesus said:
Blessed are the poor, the kingdom belongs to them.

But, dear Lord, how long must we wait for this promise to come true?
How long, O Lord, how long?

Leslie Griffiths

74

102 Te Deum (3)

The inglorious company of prisoners praise thee;
We too acknowledge thee to be the Lord.

Britain's prison population has risen inexorably in recent years. We heard 47,000 (the total number of prisoners in 1993) referred to as "alarmingly high" but have watched helplessly as that figure has risen inexorably. 51,000 in 1994 became 57,000 in 1996 and 70,000 by the end of the century is being confidently predicted.

The rhetoric of public discourse on the subject of our penal system increasingly emphasises the punitive at the expense of the rehabilitative. Many of those who linger in jails will be confirmed in their criminality by their experience inside. Custodial sentences are more and more being given when, one suspects, other forms of punishment could achieve the same or better results.

And when the prison door shuts, the tiny space within which a prisoner passes well over twenty hours in every twenty four, represents a world contracted to the tiniest span. The British public protests fiercely on behalf of cooped up chickens and crated calves but seems happy enough with the notion of factory-farmed human beings. Prisons are too often places where we can project our vindictiveness onto others. They are vile, drug-dominated, offensive places. The availability of in-cell toilets and colour televisions can never soften this hard reality.

Yet so many prisoners here and all over the world somehow manage to hang on to their dignity. They remain human beings despite all those forces that threaten to consume them.

William Wordsworth wrote a sonnet to Toussaint Louverture, leader of the Haitian slaves fighting for independence from their French masters. Toussaint was tricked by his enemies who invited him to negotiations and took him instead into captivity. The black leader died a slow and cold death in prison in the Jura Alps in April 1803 just a few months before Haiti's final victory against the forces of Napoleon Bonaparte.

Toussaint, the most unhappy man of men!
Whether the whistling rustic tend his plough
Within thy hearing, or thy head be now
Pillowed in some deep dungeon's earless den:–
O miserable Chieftain! where and when
Wilt thou find patience? Yet die not; do thou
Wear rather in thy bonds a cheerful brow:
Though fallen thyself, never to rise again,
Live and take comfort. Thou has left behind
Powers that will work for thee; air, earth, and skies;
There's not a breathing of the common wind
That will forget thee; thou hast great allies:
Thy friends are exultations, agonies,
And love, and man's unconquerable mind.

For Toussaint, read Mandela.
Behind Toussaint and Mandela
Remember all those cast into prison unjustly,
Tortured,
Starved,
Isolated,
Lonely and afraid,
Sanity stretched to breaking point,
Bodies broken,
Hope squeezed dry.

We the goodly fellowship of prisoners unite to praise thee O God;
We too acknowledge thee to be the Lord.

The Spirit of the Lord is upon me because he has chosen me to bring good news to the poor, to proclaim liberty to the captives, to set free the oppressed.

But, dear Lord, how long must we wait for this vision to come true?
How long, O Lord, how long?

Leslie Griffiths

103   Te Deum (4)

The ignoble army of the alienated praise thee;
From right around the globe they acknowledge thee.

Broken in pieces all asunder,
　Lord, hunt me not,
　A thing forgot,
Once a poor creature, now a wonder,
　A wonder tortured in the space
Betwixt this world and that of grace.

All my attendants are at strife,
　Quitting their place
　Unto my face:
Nothing performs the task of life:
　The elements are let loose to fight,
And while I live, try out their right.

[George Herbert: Affliction]

We live in a structure of contradictions,
the many facets of erstwhile unity shattered
into a million fragments.

We are in conflict with nature,
estranged from our fellows,
alienated from the essence of our own selves,
separated from God.

What is this strange and uncouth thing?
To make me sigh, and seek, and faint, and die
Until I had some place, where I might sing,
　And serve thee; and not only I,
But all my wealth, and family might combine
To set thy honour up, as our design.

Ah my dear Father, ease my smart!
These contrarieties crush me: these cross actions
Do wind a rope about, and cut my heart:
　And yet since these thy contradictions
Are properly felt by thy Son,
With but four words, my words, Thy will be done.

[George Herbert: The Cross]

We praise thee O God, our voice rises above our alienation,
and we acknowledge thee to be the Lord.

Remember that we were once without Christ,
aliens from the commonwealth and
strangers to the promises,
having no hope and without God in the world.
But now, in Christ Jesus,
we who once were far off
have been brought near
by the blood of Christ.

For he is our peace;
for those of us who were a far way off
and also for those who were near
he has broken down
the middle wall of partition
and destroyed
the hostility between (and within) us.
So we are no longer strangers and aliens
but citizens with the saints
and members of the household of God.

[from Ephesians ch.2, REB]

We therefore pray thee help thy servants,
whom thou has redeemed with thy precious blood.

How long, O Lord, how long?

Leslie Griffiths

104   Te Deum (5)

**The noble army of martyrs praise thee
And acknowledge thee to be the Lord.**

*If it should happen one day – and it could be today –
that I become a victim of the terrorism which now seems ready to encompass
all the foreigners living in Algeria,
I would like my community, my Church, my family,
to remember that my life was* **given** *to God and to this country,
I ask them to accept that the One Master of all life
was not a stranger to this brutal departure.*

*I know the scorn with which Algerians as a whole can be regarded.
I know also the caricature of Islam which a certain kind of idealism encourages.
For me, Algeria and Islam are something different: they are a body and a soul.
I have proclaimed it often enough, I believe, in the sure knowledge of what I have received from it,
finding there so often that true strand of the Gospel
learnt at my mother's knee, my very first Church,
in Algeria itself in the respect of believing Muslims.
My death, clearly, will appear to justify those who hastily judged me naive or idealistic:*

*"Let him tell us now what he thinks of it!"
But these people must realise that my most avid curiosity will then be satisfied.
This is what I shall be able to do, if God wills –
immerse my gaze in that of the Father,
to contemplate with him his children of Islam just as he sees them,
all shining with the glory of Christ,
the fruit of his Passion,
filled with the Gift of the Spirit,
whose secret joy will always be
to establish communion and to refashion the likeness,
delighting in the differences.*

*For this life given up, totally mine and totally theirs,
I thank God who seems to have wished it entirely for the sake of that* **joy**
in everything and in spite of everything.

In this **thank you***, which is said for everything in my life from now on,
I certainly include you, friends of yesterday and today,
and you my friends in this place,
along with my mother and father, my brothers and sisters and their families –
the hundredfold granted as was promised!
And you also, the friend of my final moment, who would not be aware of what you were doing.*

Yes, for you also I wish this **thank you** *– and this* **adieu** *– to commend you to the God
whose face I see in yours.
And may we find each other, happy "good thieves", in Paradise,
if it pleases God, the Father of us both.* **Amen.**

These words were were written by Fr Christian de Chergé, Superior of a Trappist monastery in Algeria, in the anticipation of his death at the hands of Moslem extremists. They were written in December 1993. Fr Christian was killed with six other members of his community in June 1996.

The blood of the martyrs is the seed of the Church.
How long, O God, how long?

Leslie Griffiths

105   Te Deum (6)

We praise thee, O God, we acknowledge thee to be the Lord.
All the earth doth worship thee, the Father everlasting.
To thee all angels cry aloud, the heavens and all the powers therein.
To thee cherubim and seraphim continually do cry:

Holy, holy, holy, Lord God of Sabaoth;
Heaven and earth are full of the majesty of thy glory.

The glorious company of the homeless were made by thee;
The goodly fellowship of the poor are all thy sons and daughters;
To thee belong all prisoners, their voices reach thy throne;
Thine too are all those alienated and also the oppressed;
The noble army of martyrs worship and praise thy holy name;
All these, the poor, the wretched of the earth, together with
The Holy Church throughout all the world acknowledge thee

The Father of an infinite majesty,
Thine honourable, true and only Son,
Also the Holy Ghost, the Comforter;

For ever and ever, till time is no more; Alleluia, Amen.

Leslie Griffiths

106   Come, Holy Spirit, and show us what is true

Come, Holy Spirit, and show us what is true.
In a world of great wealth
where many go hungry
and fortunes are won and lost
by trading in money,
Come, Holy Spirit, and show us what is true.

In a world of great knowledge
where many die of ignorance
and every piece of information
has a price in the marketplace,
Come, Holy Spirit, and show us what is true.

In a world of easy communication
where words leap between continents
and we expect to see a picture
to illustrate each item of news,
Come, Holy Spirit, and show us what is true.

In a church touched by the flame of Pentecost
moved to generous sacrifice and costly love
interpreting the will of God with new insight
Come, Holy Spirit, and show us what is true.

Stephen Orchard

107 Magnificat

Leader: My soul proclaims the greatness of the Lord
All: **My spirit rejoices in God my Saviour.**

Voice 1: As he called Mary, a scrap of a girl, to mother his only son, so he seems to notice nobodies like you and me, inviting us to work with him to build a better world.

Leader: My soul proclaims the greatness of the Lord
All: **My spirit rejoices in God my Saviour.**

Voice 1: The almighty God, lord of all power and might, awesome in holiness, has favoured a simple woman with his grace. He has made her his partner in the offer of salvation he extends to all people in every generation.

Leader: My soul proclaims the greatness of the Lord
All: **My spirit rejoices in God my Saviour.**

Voice 2: His mercy is free and boundless, it remains constant and unshaken, it liberates captive spirits in every age. The taste of God's mercy fills the heart with life and hope and peace and joy.

Leader: He has showed strength with his arm
All: **His mercy is on those who fear him.**

Voice 2: Human pride has no place in his presence.
Those who trust their own power delude themselves.
The humble stand taller in God's eyes than the proud,
It's not the powerful he blesses but the meek.

Leader: He has showed strength with his arm
All: **His mercy is on those who fear him.**

Voice 1: He has filled the hungry with good things; in them we find his blessings; in feeding them we honour those whom God has already honoured; in neglecting them we turn our backs on God himself.

Leader: My soul proclaims the greatness of the Lord
All: **My spirit rejoices in God my Saviour.**

Voice 2: We who are rich must take heed; we have been warned; our wealth in no way wins us access to our heavenly father. To put our confidence in material things is a counsel of despair; it's from the poor we need to learn just how to trust in God through thick and thin.

Leader: My soul proclaims the greatness of the Lord
All: **My spirit rejoices in God my Saviour.**

Voice 1: God keeps his word. Great is his faithfulness. To Abraham and his descendents, to Mary, to all who take his yoke upon them, he remembers his mercy. Holy is his name.

Leader: My soul proclaims the greatness of the Lord
All: **My spirit rejoices in God my Saviour.**

Leader: Glory to the Father and to the Son and to the Holy Spirit;
All: **as it was in the beginning, is now, and shall be for ever. Amen.**

Leslie Griffiths

108   Nunc Dimittis

O Lord now lettest thou thy servant depart in peace......

In peace. Yes peace.
Peace.
But a century studded with wars
tells its own and somewhat different story.
Of young men going "over the top"
into the arms of a grey and inevitable death;
lions led by donkeys into the valley of the grisly shadow;
It's been the story of Cambodian killing fields
and Sharpeville massacre.
It tells of a world where Tamil tigers, Contra rebels,
Frelimo and Renamo brothers and sisters
have engaged in bloody internecine strife
armed to the teeth with weapons Made in Britain.
A hundred years of scattered wars has seen the Falklands/Malvinas,
the Burma Road, Pearl Harbour strung
like dull beads on a long necklace together with
Hiroshima and Nagasaki, Rwanda and Bosnia,
Vietnam, Korea and the suffering of East Timor,
Armenia, Afghanistan, Algeria, Angola
to keep them company.
And then the Holocaust
on its own
heavy with the silent eloquence of the six million.
And so on and so forth forever and ever.
Amen?
No. Surely not amen.

How many old men like Simeon,
        old women like Anna,
have seen the worst and yet still long for the best,
have lived through wars and hatred
yet still yearn to depart in peace?
Our old men dream dreams of how things might have been,
        might still be.
Dear old Simeon, almost ready to go, but not without his final word,
his word of hope for posterity.

Mine eyes have seen thy salvation
which thou hast prepared for all people......

For all people. For *all* people.
For the least, the last, the lost, for all people.

Salvation,
wholeness,
shalom,
peace,
for all people.

That, and nothing less than that, is your plan dear Lord.
And yet it's so at odds
With what we see and live with
Day after day,
Week after week,
Year after year,
Till the last syllable of recorded time.
And all our yesterdays have surely lighted more fools
the way to dusty death than dogs have dinners.
For all your plan, life is too often
a tale told by veritable idiots,
full of sound and fury,
signifying nothing in particular,
little more than the chronicle of human greed and cruelty
till the last syllable of recorded time.

Oh people you shall not drown in your tears
But tears shall bathe your wounds.

Oh people, you shall not die from hunger
But hunger shall feed your souls.

Oh people, you are not weak in your suffering
But strong and brave with knowing.

Oh people, if you have known struggle
Only then are you capable of loving.

O people be aware of the love you have.
Let not your tears submerge it
Let not your hunger eat it
Let not your suffering destroy it.

Oh people, bitterness does not replace a grain of love.

Let us be awake in our love.   *[Noorie Cassim, South Africa]*

To be a light to lighten the Gentiles.....

Dear Simeon,
shaking Israel out of its isolationist stance,
refusing to equate election with apartheid,
        or to make chosen-ness into exclusivism,
        God-with-us into God-with-us-and-only-us.

Israel's vocation is to be light for everyone,
Theirs is a calling to hold out God's peace
to the world
        to the whole world
                and nothing but the whole world,
and to call all the nations of the world
to enjoy that *shalom* which defies understanding,
the deep peace of the running wave and the whispering breeze.

Instead of which.....
Suffering peoples inflict suffering on others,
Chosen peoples cling to their chosen-ness at any expense
The elect snuff out the light which God has lit in them for the benefit of all.

81

Dear Lord,
> turn our religions inside out,
> save them all from the modes of self glorification,
> make servanthood the hallmark of their authenticity,
> show all believing people
>> that the secret,
>> the source,
>> the origin
> of all that's worth having and striving for
> has already been modelled for us
> in the self-sacrificing love of Jesus.

Help us to give ourselves to others so that with Simeon we may offer light for all the nations, light in our day. Teach us that then, and only then, will our religious belief catch flame and reveal.......**the glory of thy people Israel.**

Glory be to the Father and to the Son and to the Holy Spirit;
As it was in the beginning as now and shall be for ever. Amen.

Leslie Griffiths

109   Sanctus

Holy, holy, holy Lord,

we praise you with words
we acknowledge you in the silence of our deepest being

God of power and might.

Heaven – its distances and its galaxies
and earth – its beauty and diversity

are full of your glory,
Hosanna in the highest.

We praise you for giving us your Son, our Lord Jesus Christ,
who redeems our love from selfishness
and inspires us to all that is noble and true,

Blessed is he who comes in the name of the Lord.

And we thank you too for your Holy Spirit
who makes us one with each other and with you,
who holds us together as one human family
spread to all the corners of the world.

Hosanna in the highest.

We offer our prayer to you
our one and only God
in the name of Jesus
and through the power of the Holy Spirit

Amen.

Leslie Griffiths

110   The Horrors of our History

1   The horrors of our history
        are vast, beyond belief.
    We greet each new atrocity
        with bafflement, or grief,
    yet all the evil energies
        that haunt the human race,
    come, not from alien galaxies,
        but from our inner space,
        and terror, pain and genocide
        intrude on every prayer,
        with shades that whisper,
            "Where is God?
                If only God were there!"

2   By torture, war and poverty,
        by flame and firing squad,
    for glory, flag and destiny,
        and with a prayer to God,
    God's image finds a thousand ways
        to torment, and to kill
    and asks how love can justify
        such terrible freewill:
        for every cry of suffering
        will drive us back to prayer,
        as thousands clamour,
            "Where is God?
                If only God were there!"

3   Yet if, like some robotic race,
        though warm with flesh and blood,
    our happy self, with smiling face,
        was programmed to be good,
    and had no freedom, seeing wrong,
        to seek it, or say no,
    our praise would be a puppet-song,
        and love, and empty show.
        Our pain and terror mark the cost
        of every faithful prayer
        that chooses justice,
        love, and trust,
            and hopes that God is there.

4   And God is not an analyst,
        observing gain and loss,
    but loves us to the uttermost
        and suffers on a cross:
    for love comes, not like Heads of State,
        in power and glamour known,
    but as a loser, desolate,
        in anguish, and alone:
        the cross, revealed in Easter light,
        will nourish every prayer
        when faith discovers,
            "There is God,
                and all of God is there!"

5   The fruits of knowledge, plucked and prized,
        have scattered wide their seed:
    we are as gods, with open eyes,
        for shame or glory freed,
    and share, as midwives to our God,
        the work of giving birth
    to faith's fulfilment, mercy's child:
        new heavens and new earth.
        Come blow, great wind of Pentecost,
        till all the churches dare
        to bear the horrors,
            heal the wounds,
                and show that God is there!

Brian Wren

111 A Litany for use in Times of National Crisis

Leader: Almighty God, whose is the eternal only power, and all other power but borrowed from you: we pray earnestly for all those who hold power that, holding it first from you, they may use it for the general good and for your honour: through Jesus Christ our Lord.

All: **Amen.**

Leader: What does the Lord require of you but to do justly, to love mercy, and to walk humbly with your God?

Lord have mercy upon us.

All: **Christ have mercy upon us.**

Leader: Lord have mercy upon us.

From greed and selfishness; from envy and covetousness, from pride and contempt; from injustice and oppression,

All: **Good Lord, deliver us.**

Leader: From love of money, which is the root of all kinds of evil; from trust in riches, and from regarding human life as consisting in the abundance of the things we possess,

All: **Good Lord, deliver us.**

Leader: From unjust dealings and dishonest practices; from seeking gain without merit, and especially if this is at someone else's expense; from profit in things hurtful to other people; and from selling our own souls for material gain,

All: **Good Lord, deliver us.**

Leader: From the spirit of contention; from bitterness and hatred; and from all denial of our common humanity and of one-ness in Christ,

All: **Good Lord, deliver us.**

Leader: Deliver your Church, O Lord, from the worship of money, from bondage to the world, and from all complicity in social evil and from silence in the presence of wrong;

All: **We beg you to hear us, good Lord.**

Leader: For all who are anxious about their future, all who are out of work, all who are in want and despair,

All: **We beg you to hear us, good Lord.**

Leader: That you will raise up deliverance for the poor and heavy-laden, for the defenceless and oppressed, and for all whose labour is without joy; that all your people may taste the glorious liberty of the children of God,

All: **We beg you to hear us, good Lord.**

Leader: Finally, we implore you, in whom all honest work is wrought and to whom all worthy service is rendered, to guide, protect and inspire all who labour for the means of life;

All: **Hear us, Lord, hear us we pray.**

Leader: That they may be faithful in service, honest in craftsmanship, diligent in business, just and understanding in the control of others,

All: **Hear us, Lord, hear us we pray.**

Leader: That you will guide with your wisdom all those to whom is committed the government of the nation, that they may truly serve you in the ordering of our social life,

All: **Hear us, Lord, hear us we pray.**

Leader: That you will bless all who labour to heal sickness and relieve distress,

All: **Hear us, Lord, hear us we pray.**

Leader: That you will inspire and enlighten all teachers, all men and women of science and learning, art and literature, and all who help form public opinion,

All: **Hear us, Lord, hear us we pray.**

Leader: That your blessing may rest upon all who work at home and have the care of little children,

All: **Hear us, Lord, hear us we pray.**

Leader: Hasten, O Lord, the day when all people will toil not merely for their own gain but for the common good; when all government shall be compassionate and just, when all commerce pure, all labour prayer, all work worship, and when men and women shall rejoice in the things they do and find increase of wealth in mutual service; through Jesus Christ our Lord,

All: **Amen.**

Leslie Griffiths

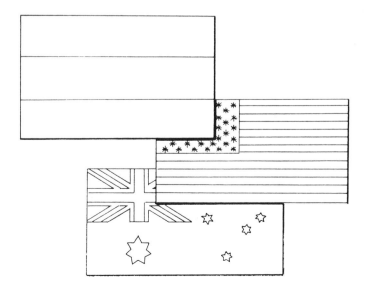

85

The Future

112 A Litany for Times of Darkness

O God our Father in heaven, have mercy upon us,
Have mercy upon us we pray.

O Christ, only Son of the Father, have mercy upon us,
Have mercy upon us we pray.

Holy Spirit, giver of life and hope, have mercy upon us,
Have mercy upon us we pray.

Holy, blessed, and glorious trinity; Father, Son and Holy Spirit,
have mercy on us.
Have mercy upon us we pray.

* * * * *

As we hold up a world where pain and needless suffering are the daily experience of so many people,
Hear us, good Lord, we implore you.

That it may please you to reveal your will in situations of distress and despair,
Hear us, good Lord, we implore you.

For peoples who've lived with the bitter experience of war and who now have to live with the legacy of strife,
Hear us, good Lord, we implore you.

For politicians who face the task of rebuilding shattered economies, reconstituting scattered communities,
Hear us, good Lord, we implore you.

For all those seeking to clear the way for a safer future by redefining the role of armies, calling in guns and other weapons of destruction,
Hear us, good Lord, we implore you.

For those who go on supplying the poorest countries of the world with arms;
- heavy arms like tanks and missiles,
- complicated arms like automatic weapons and radar systems,
- landmines galore, 12 million in Angola, more in Cambodia, and also in Afghanistan,

Hear us, good Lord, we implore you.

For those who carry the scars of war;
Hear us, good Lord, we implore you.

For the scores of thousands who've lost arms and legs, the countless people whose houses and businesses have been destroyed by bombs and fire, familes who've suffered the death or mutilation of loved ones;
Hear us, good Lord, we implore you.

For unknown numbers who cry themselves to sleep each night,
Hear us, good Lord, we implore you.

For agencies and non-governmental organisations that seek to stand alongside the poor, to bring an end to conflict, to equip people for survival and the eventual re-fashioning of their lives,
Hear us, good Lord, we implore you.

* * * * *

O God, we have heard with our ears, and our fathers and mothers have told us of the noble things you did in their days and in the days long ago before them.
O Lord, arise, help us, and deliver us now in the day of our need.

From our enemies and the enemies of humanity defend us, O Christ.
Graciously look upon our afflictions.

Pitifully look on the sorrows in the hearts of all those you have made in your own image.
Mercifully break the power of sin over our lives.

Favourably with mercy hear our prayers.
Son of David, have mercy upon us.

O Lord, let your mercy be shown in our lives.
Let them be transformed by your love.

Almighty God, you who have given us grace at this time with one accord to make our common supplications to you, you who have promised that where two or three are gathered together in your name you will grant their requests; fulfil now, O Lord, the desires and petitions of your servants, as may be most expedient for them; granting us in this world knowledge of your truth, and in the world to come life everlasting. **Amen.**

Leslie Griffiths

113 CAFOD Millenium Prayer

God of all ages, Lord of all time,
you are the Alpha and the Omega,
the origin and goal of everything that lives,
yet you are ever close to those
who call on you in faith.

We look with expectant joy
to the Jubilee of your Son's coming among us,
two thousand years ago.
We thank you for the years of favour
with which you have blessed your people.

Teach us to share justly the good things
which come from your loving hand;
to bring peace and reconciliation
where strife and disorder reign;
to speak out as advocates
for those who have no voice;
and to rejoice in a bond of prayer and praise
with our sisters and brothers throughout the world.

When Christ comes again in glory,
may he find us alive and active in faith,
and so call us to that Kingdom
where, with you and the Holy Spirit,
he is God, to be praised, worshipped and glorified,
both now and for ages to come. **Amen.**

114 Transfiguring Hope

TRANSFIGURING HOPE

Alison Harker (1949–) and Ian Harker (1939–)

Optional instruments or vocalise

1 Where there is darkness, let there be loving,
where there is doubting, let there be joy;
cry 'Hosanna', shout 'Hallelujah',
turn a world of hunger into a harvest of hope.

2 Where there is sickness, let there be healing,
where there is dying, let there be faith;
cry 'Hosanna', shout 'Hallelujah',
turn a world of grieving into a promise of hope.

3 Where there is anger, let there be justice,
where there is discord, let there be peace;
cry 'Hosanna', shout 'Hallelujah',
turn a world of chaos into a commune of hope.

4 Where there is squalor, let there be beauty,
where there is darkness, let there be light;
cry 'Hosanna', shout 'Hallelujah',
turn a world of strangers into the family of hope.

5 Where there is warfare, let there be judgement,
where there is suffering, let there be wrath;
cry 'Hosanna', shout 'Hallelujah',
turn the whole creation into transfiguring hope.

Brian Frost and Lucy Griffiths

90

115 Praying for a Change

Reader 1:   **It is not true** that we must accept inhumanity and discrimination, hunger and poverty, death and destruction.

Reader 2:   **This is true:** I have come that they may have life and have it abundantly.

Reader 1:   **It is not true** that we are simply victims of the powers of evil that seek to rule the world.

Reader 2:   **This is true:** To me is given all authority in heaven and on earth, and lo, I am with you always, even to the end of the age.

Reader 1:   **It is not true** that we have to wait for those who are specially gifted, who are the prophets of the church, before we can do anything.

Reader 2:   **This is true:** I will pour out my spirit on all flesh, and your sons and daughters will prophecy, and your old men shall dream dreams and your young men shall see visions.

Reader 1:   **It is not true** that our dreams for the liberation of humankind and our dreams for justice, of human dignity, of peace, are not meant for this earth and for this history.

Reader 2:   **This is true:** The hour comes and it is now, that true worshippers shall worship the Father in spirit and in truth.

Reader 1:   We pray as Jesus taught us, that God's will be done on earth as it is in heaven:

All: **Our Father.......Amen.**

Allan A. Boesak

116 Sons and Daughters of Creation

VERONICA (8.7.8.7.8.7. Trochaic)

Derek Scott (1921–)

Sons and daugh-ters of cre-a-tion by God's will_ we_ came to be.

Like a po-et dream-ing mar-vels he has spun our his-to-ry,

work-ing, till from shape-less cha-os he e-voked hu-man-i-ty.

1 Sons and daughters of creation
by God's will we came to be.
Like a poet dreaming marvels
he has spun our history,
working, till from shapeless chaos
he evoked humanity.

2 Dark within our first conceiving
run the rifts that still divide:
envy splits and anger hardens,
colour, gender, wealth collide:
sov'reign nations arm for conflict,
violence thrusting peace aside.

3 Yet God holds his steadfast purpose
of humanity made one.
Walls were breached and bounds transcended
by the death of his own Son:
and the way for love's encounter
through the Spirit's power begun.

4 Down the restless generations,
called of God, his church has grown.
Martyrs' heirs and prophets' children
penetrated lands unknown,
challenged by unlikeness, finding
gifts to complement their own.

5 Now as partners in one mission,
we must share across the earth
hope of what God will accomplish,
faith that promises new birth
to the selves that sin has shattered,
love restoring each life's worth.

6 Rich from all that we inherit,
strong with skills new worlds devise,
Father, may we serve your Kingdom;
under crisis-clouded skies,
confidently reaffirming
where the morning's glory lies.

Michael Hare Duke

117 Take Possession of our Hearts

Prayers of intercession used at Wesley's Chapel, September 1st 1996, with the response, in full, being a prayer by John Wesley.

Take possession of our hearts, O Lord,
That being created by you, we may ever live for you.

Creator, Alpha and Omega,
God of beginnings and endings,
our prayers begin where we are –
in this congregation, with those who are beginning
a new ministry in a new place,
with those who take on new responsibilities,
those for whom beginnings are also endings,
with all worshipping here for the first time,
and with the whole people of God
at the beginning of a new year....

Take possession of our hearts, O Lord,
That being created by you, we may ever live for you.

God with us, who in Jesus Christ
shared our daily lives, be with those
for whom Monday and the week ahead
will mark a new beginning – in school, at work, in a new home;
for the families of ministers
and the staff who serve the whole church;
for those beginning again in other ways,
young people leaving home,
those leaving prison, or hospital,
or facing life after bereavement.

Take possession of our hearts, O Lord,
That being created by you, we may ever live for you.

Spirit of new life, of fragile hope,
springing afresh in our hearts,
may we see you at work
in those places which cry out for resurrection:
in Rwanda and Burundi, in Israel and Iraq......(etc),
in prisons and palaces,
in refugee camps and women's refuges,
may justice and peace come, hand in hand,
and wherever there is pain, anger, confusion,
may hearts be warmed and lives changed.

Take possession of our hearts, O Lord,
that being created by you, we may ever live for you;
that being created for you,
we may ever act for your glory;
and being redeemed by you
we may ever render to you what is yours. Amen.

Jan Sutch Pickard

118 Keep a Light in your Eyes for the Children of the World

KEEP A LIGHT IN YOUR EYES

Ruth Thomas (1956–)

Keep a light in your eyes for the child-ren of the world_ for the

1. child-ren of the world,_ for the child-ren. Keep a

2. child-ren of the world need

you. Keep a can-dle burn-ing, burn-ing, burn-ing, Keep a can-dle

burning, burning, burning, Keep a can-dle burning, burning, burning, for the children of the world.

1 Keep a light in your eyes for the children of the world
for the children of the world, for the children.
Keep a light in your eyes for the children of the world
for the children of the world need you.
Keep a candle burning, burning, burning,
keep a candle burning, burning, burning,
keep a candle burning, burning, burning,
for the children of the world.

2 Keep strength in your heart for the children of the world
for the children of the world, for the children.
Keep strength in your heart for the children of the world
for the children of the world need you.
Chorus

3 Keep a song on your lips for the children of the world
for the children of the world, for the children.
Keep a song on your lips for the children of the world
for the children of the world need you.
Chorus

4 Light a candle in the minds of the children of the world
of the children of the world, of the children.
Light a candle in the minds of the children of the world
for the children of the world need you.
Chorus

Ruth Thomas

95

119   Peace is my Parting Gift to you

"Peace is my parting gift to you.

Go in Peace:
  not as the world gives;
    not in pretending;
      not in submitting;
        not in possessing;
          not in the glory of winning,
            the fever of getting.

For Peace is my parting gift to you.

    Go in Peace:
      as the makers of peace;
      as the shakers of wrong;
      as the people of God,
    singing a peacable song.
    Go in Peace."

Brian Wren

120   Dismissal (after Communion)

Go in peace
With a song in your heart
For the God of peace
Is with you.

Leslie Griffiths

Acknowledgements

The publishers are grateful to the following for permission to reproduce their material in this publication. The acknowledgements are listed in numerical order of the items in the book. Every effort has been made to trace copyright holders but in a few cases this has proved impossible. In the event of those listed untraced coming forward, we will be pleased to make due acknowledgement in any reprint.

Number	Author	Copyright Holder/Source
1	Leslie Griffiths	Stainer & Bell Ltd
2	–	© The Trustees for Methodist Church Purposes. From *Methodist Prayer Handbook 1996–97*. Used by permission of the Methodist Publishing House.
3	–	© The Trustees for Methodist Church Purposes. From *Setting the Word on Fire*, Methodist Conference 1996. Main prayers used by permission of the Methodist Publishing House. The reponse is adapted from Psalm 19 by Leslie Griffiths (Stainer & Bell Ltd).
4	Alan Gaunt	Stainer & Bell Ltd
5	June Baker	Stainer & Bell Ltd & The Trustees for Methodist Church Purposes
6	Leslie Griffiths	Stainer & Bell Ltd
7(i)	Leslie Griffiths	Stainer & Bell Ltd
7(ii)	Unknown	Source untraced
7(iii)	Unknown	Source untraced
7(iv)	Unknown	Source untraced
8	Leslie Griffiths	Stainer & Bell Ltd
9	Leslie Griffiths	Stainer & Bell Ltd
10	–	Used by permission of the South African Council of Churches, PO Box 4921, Johannesburg 2000.
11	Andrew Pratt	Stainer & Bell Ltd
12(text)	Alec Davison	Stainer & Bell Ltd
12(music)	Tony Biggin	Stainer & Bell Ltd
13	Hans Küng	From *Judaism* (pp. 581/2) translated John Bowden, SCM Press 1992. Used by permission of SCM Press, London and The Continuum Publishing Company, New York.
14	–	From *Ghana: Heart of Prayer. African, Jewish and Biblical Prayers* edited A. Gittins. Owner untraced.
15	Anonymous	Source untraced
16	–	From *I Lie on My Mat and Pray: Prayers by Young Africans*, edited by Fritz Pawelzik, translated by Robbins Strong. © 1964 Friendship Press, New York. Used by permission.
17	Anonymous	Source untraced
18	–	From *A Generous Land*. Used by permission of CAFOD, Christian Aid, SCIAF and Trocaire.
19	Rigoberta Menchu	Untraced
20	–	From *I Sing Your Praise All the Day Long: Young Africans at Prayer*, edited by Fritz Pawelzik. © 1967 Friendship Press, New York. Used by permission.
21	–	From *The World at One in Prayer* by Daniel J. Fleming. © 1942 Harper & Row Publishers Inc. © Renewed 1970. Used by permission of HarperCollins Publishers Inc, New York.
22	Chinua Achebe	From *No Longer at Ease*. Heinemann Educational Books. Used by permission.
23	Trevor Huddleston	From *For All God's People*. World Council of Churches, Geneva. Used by permission.
24	–	'Prayer for our Country' from *A Book of Common Prayer, CPSA*. © Provincial Trustees of the Church of the Province of Southern Africa. Used by permission.
25	–	From *Uniting in Hope*. WCC Publications, Geneva. Used by permission.
26	Dom Hélder Cámara	English translation © World Council of Churches, Geneva. Used by permission.
27	Ernesto Cardenal	By permission of the author and the World Council of Churches, Geneva for the English translation.
28 and 29	–	From *The World at One in Prayer* by Daniel J. Fleming. © 1942 Harper & Row Publishers Inc. © Renewed 1970. Used by permission of HarperCollins Publishers Inc, New York.
30	Emilio Castro	By permission of the World Council of Churches, Geneva on behalf of the author. From *For All God's People*.
31	Reinhold Niebuhr	From World Student Christian Federation book of prayers *Adoremus II*, revised edition.
32	Leslie Brandt	From *Psalms Now*. © 1974 Concordia Publishing House, USA. Used by permission.
33	Patrick Prescod	© 1981 Caribbean Conference of Churches (CCC). All rights reserved. Used by permssion of the CCC.
34	Léopold Sédar Senghor	From *Selected Poems*, translated by John Reed and Clive Wake. © 1964 Oxford University Press. Used by permission.
35	Rabbi Nachman of Bratzlav	By permission of Leo Baeck College, 80 East End Road, London N3 2SY
36(music)	Hannah Daniels	Stainer & Bell Ltd
36(text)	Andrew Pratt	Stainer & Bell Ltd
37	John Pritchard	By permission of the author.

38	Anonymous	Source untraced
39	–	Used by permission of the South African Council of Churches, PO Box 4921, Johannesburg 2000.
40	Leslie Griffiths	Stainer & Bell Ltd
41	Leslie Griffiths	Stainer & Bell Ltd
42	–	From *Ghana, Heart of Prayer: African, Jewish and Biblical Prayers* edited A. Gittins. Owner untraced.
43	Peggy M. de Cuehlo	Untraced
44	Leslie Griffiths	Stainer & Bell Ltd
45	Sanja Matešic	By permission of the author.
46	Radovan Karadzic	From *There's a Miracle* (1982) as quoted in *The Guardian*, July 13 1996. Untraced.
47(music)	Mervyn Horder	Stainer & Bell Ltd
47(text)	Christopher Idle	Stainer & Bell Ltd/Christopher Idle for the world except USA and Canada and Hope Publishing Company for USA and Canada.
48	Leslie Griffiths	Stainer & Bell Ltd
49	Brian Wren	Stainer & Bell Ltd for the world except USA, Canada, Australia and New Zealand which are controlled by Hope Publishing Company
50(i)	Leslie Griffiths	Stainer & Bell Ltd
50(ii)	St Patrick	Public Domain
50(iii)	–	Pax Christi Ireland. Used by permission.
50(iv)	Anonymous	Source untraced
51(music)	David McCarthy	Stainer & Bell Ltd
51(text)	Alan Gaunt	Stainer & Bell Ltd
52	Leslie Griffiths	Stainer & Bell Ltd
53	Leslie Griffiths	Stainer & Bell Ltd
54	Leslie Griffiths	Stainer & Bell Ltd
55	Leslie Griffiths	Stainer & Bell Ltd
56	Leslie Griffiths	Stainer & Bell Ltd
57	Alexander Solzhenitsyn	From *Solzhenitsyn: A Pictorial Autobiography*. Owner untraced.
58	Edmund Banyard	By permission of the author.
59	Revised English Bible	© 1989 Oxford University Press and Cambridge University Press. Used by permission.
60	Philip Banyard	Stainer & Bell Ltd
61	McMurray S. Richey	By permission of Professor McMurray S. Richey and the Duke University Archives, North Carolina, USA.
62	Douglas MacArthur	Public Domain
63	Leslie Griffiths	Stainer & Bell Ltd
64	Dag Hammarskjöld	From *Markings* translated Auden/Sjoberg. Translation © 1964 Alfred A. Knopf Inc, New York and Faber & Faber Ltd, London. Reprinted by permission of the publishers.
65	Martin Israel	Untraced
66	Anonymous	Untraced
67	Tirzah ben-David	By permission of the author.
68	Leslie Griffiths	Stainer & Bell Ltd
69	June Boyce-Tillman	Stainer & Bell Ltd & Women in Theology
70	Julia Esquival	Untraced
71	Eduardo Galeano	Untraced
72	–	From *The Tablet*. Used by permission.
73(i)	Thich Nhat Hanh	Stainer & Bell Ltd
73(ii)	Charles Wesley	Public Domain
74	Donald Swann	Stainer & Bell Ltd
75	–	© 1995 The Anglican Church of Australia Trust Corporation. From the text of *A Prayer Book for Australia* published under the imprint of Broughton Books. Reproduced with permission.
76	Leslie Griffiths	Stainer & Bell Ltd
77	Leslie Griffiths	Stainer & Bell Ltd
78	Kahil Gibran	Untraced
79	Dag Hammarskjöld	From *Markings* translated Auden/Sjoberg. Translation © 1964 Alfred Knopf Inc, New York and Faber & Faber Ltd, London. Used by permission of the publishers.
80	Latin American child of 10	From *Lifelines*, Christian Aid, 1987. Used by permission of Christian Aid.
81	Cecil Rajendra	By permission of the author.
82	Karl Gaspar	From *How Long? Prison Reflections of Karl Gaspar*. Used by permission of Claretian Communications Inc, Quezon City, Philippines.
83	W. M. B. Nhlapo	Untraced
84	M. K. Ghandi	Untraced
85	Henry Vaughan	Public Domain
86	An Indian Medical Student	Source untraced
87(i)	Hilarion	Quotation from *The Russian Religious Mind* by G. P. Fedotov, Harvard University Press. Owner untraced.
87(ii)	Nikolai Berdyaev	Quotation from his essay *Spirits of the Russian Revolution*, The New Review, No. 79, 1965 (June), New York, p.222–23. Used by permission.

87(iii)	Robert Service	Quotation from article in *The Guardian* on 25th October 1997. By permission of the author.
88	Fred Pratt Green	Stainer & Bell Ltd for world except USA and Canada and Hope Publishing Company for USA and Canada.
88	Revised English Bible	© 1989 Oxford University Press and Cambridge University Press. Used by permission.
89	Gerald Manley Hopkins	Public Domain
90	J. A. Paul Booth	Stainer & Bell Ltd
91		Whole item by Angela Ashwin from *Patterns not Padlocks*. Used by permission of Eagle Publishing. Biblical quotations from *RSV* and *NRSV* by permission of Division of Christian Education of the National Council of the Churches of Christ in the USA, 475 Riverside Drive, Room 872, New York NY 10115–0050 and SPCK, London and The Crossroads Publishing Company, New York for the quotation of Mechtild of Madgeburg from *Beguine Spirituality* edited Fiona Bowie, translated Oliver Davies (SPCK, 1989).
92(text)	Christopher Idle	Stainer & Bell Ltd/Christopher Idle for world except USA and Canada and Hope Publishing Company for USA and Canada
92(music)	Mervyn Horder	Stainer & Bell Ltd
93	Leslie Griffiths	Stainer & Bell Ltd
94	Graham Cook	From *Say One for Me*, 1990 United Reformed Church Prayer Handbook. Used by permission of the author.
95	Fred Kaan	Stainer & Bell Ltd for world except USA and Canada and Hope Publishing Company for USA and Canada.
96(i)	Revised English Bible	© 1989 Oxford University Press and Cambridge University Press. Used by permission.
96(ii)	John Donne	Public Domain
96(iii)	Charles Wesley	Public Domain
96(iv)	Daniel Iverson	© 1963 Birdwing Music/EMI Christian Music Publishing. Administered by CopyCare, PO Box 77, Hailsham, BN27 3EF, UK. Used by permission.
97	Leslie Griffiths	Stainer & Bell Ltd
98(music)	Traditional German	Public Domain
98(text)	Ian Fraser	Stainer & Bell Ltd
99	Leslie Griffiths	Stainer & Bell Ltd
100	Leslie Griffiths	Stainer & Bell Ltd
100	Revised English Bible	© 1989 Oxford University Press and Cambridge University Press. Used by permission.
101	Leslie Griffths	Stainer & Bell Ltd
101	Timothy J. Mark	© Trustees for Methodist Church Purposes from *The World Calls Christians to Prayer*. Used by permission of the Methodist Publishing House.
102	Leslie Griffiths	Stainer & Bell Ltd
102	William Wordsworth	Public Domain
103	Leslie Griffiths	Stainer & Bell Ltd
103	George Herbert	Public Domain
103	Revised English Bible	© 1989 Oxford University Press and Cambridge University Press. Used by permission.
104	Leslie Griffiths	Stainer & Bell Ltd
104	Father Christian de Chergé	From *The Tablet*. Used by permission.
105	Leslie Griffiths	Stainer & Bell Ltd
106	Stephen Orchard	Used by permission of the author. From *All the Glorious Names*, United Reformed Church Prayer Handbook, 1989.
107	Leslie Griffths	Stainer & Bell Ltd
108	Leslie Griffiths	Stainer & Bell Ltd
108	Noorie Cassim	© Noorie Cassim. From *Staffrider*, March 1979. Untraced.
109	Leslie Griffiths	Stainer & Bell Ltd
110	Brian Wren	Stainer & Bell Ltd for world except USA, Canada, Australia and New Zealand which are controlled by Hope Publishing Company
111	Leslie Griffiths	Stainer & Bell Ltd
112	Leslie Griffiths	Stainer & Bell Ltd
113	–	Used by permission of CAFOD, Romero Close, Stockwell Road, London SW9 9TY
114(text)	Brian Frost/Lucy Griffiths	Stainer & Bell Ltd
114(music)	Ian and Alison Harker	Stainer & Bell Ltd
115	Allan A. Boesak	Extract from presentation by Allan A. Boesak to WCC VI Assembly, on the theme *Jesus Christ, the Life of the World*. In *Gathered for Life: Official Report*, WCC VI Assembly, Vancouver, Canada, 1983, Ed. David Gill, © 1983 WCC Publications, Geneva, Switzerland. Used by permission.
116(text)	Michael Hare Duke	Stainer & Bell Ltd
116(music)	Derek Scott	Stainer & Bell Ltd
117	Jan Sutch Pickard	© The Trustees for Methodist Church Purposes. Used by permission of the Methodist Publishing House.
118	Ruth Thomas	Stainer & Bell Ltd and The Trustees for Methodist Church Purposes
119	Brian Wren	Stainer & Bell Ltd for world except USA, Canada, Australia and New Zealand which are controlled by Hope Publishing Company
120	Leslie Griffiths	Stainer & Bell Ltd

Index of Persons

This index excludes Leslie Griffiths, whose mark is on the whole anthology, but includes people mentioned in or contributing to the book.

Index of Places

Select Index of Themes

A particular strength of this book is the use of a wide vocabulary conveying the subtle differences that exist in situations of a similar but diverse nature. In general this select index follows the diverse vocabulary and readers should look under several theme words to find the material that is significant for a particular occasion.